Major League Life

Why Major League Lacrosse Players, Coaches, and Fans Share a Passion for a League That Often Goes Overlooked

Phil Shore

DEDICATION

To my wife, Brooke, for pushing me to pursue my passion project, being my travel agent and booking most of my trips, holding down the fort when I was away, listening to my stories, and providing your support and love.

CONTENTS

Acknowledgments   i

Introduction   1

1   New York at Boston   4

2   Dallas at Atlanta   17

3   Chesapeake at Denver   30

4   Boston at Dallas   44

5   New York at Chesapeake   65

6   MLL All-Star Game   79

7   Atlanta at New York   91

8   MLL Championship Weekend   102

Final Words   114

ACKNOWLEDGMENTS

I would like to thank all the individuals that agreed to be interviewed for this book. It is a pleasure to share your stories.

I would like to thank all the league and team PR contacts that helped me set up these interviews: Carrie Gamper, Tyler Englander, Keller Dinan, Spencer Ford, Marcus Williams, Grant Larson, Austin Lee, Lisa LaPlaca, Heather Huntemann, and Jody Fisher. You treated me well and helped me get everything I envisioned and more.

I would like to thank all of the editors I've worked with in my time as a journalist. Thank you for all the opportunities you've afforded me to write and for helping me improve my craft.

I would like to thank my coaches and teammates for helping me learn and enjoy the sport of lacrosse.

I would like to thank my family – especially my dad, mom, brothers, and sister – and friends for all of their encouragement.

I would like to thank my wife, Brooke, for always being so amazing, and my dog, Jersey, for always excitedly greeting me when I came home from my trips.

I would like to thank you, the reader, for giving this book a chance.

INTRODUCTION

"The MLL is straight up the lacrosse D league now."

"Hate to say it but the MLL has no shot, PLL is doing the things MLL should have been doing ten years ago."

"MLL may have lost me today."

"I can't wait for you to fail now #ripmachine"

"Columbus Ohio really could use a team again now that the other shitty league decided [sic] to end our team here."

"This is an absolute JOKE of an organization. I hope the PLL washes this sorry excuse of a professional league away."

"The talent is not split, it's not even close. The PLL is head and shoulders above the MLL."

"The @MLL_Lacrosse is feeling the heat. This statement proves it. I had serious doubts about the PLL. I was wrong, again. MLL looks like they have a bunch of elementary media kids running their games. PLL & NBC have set the bar too high for the MLL to survive."

"The MLL is dead long live the @PremierLacrosse."

These quotes are a small sample of comments made across social media regarding the professional field lacrosse landscape at the end of 2018 and throughout 2019.

MLL stands for Major League Lacrosse, the oldest men's professional field lacrosse league in the United States. It was founded in 1999 by Jake Steinfeld (of Body By Jake fame), Dave Morrow, and Tim Robertson. The league's inaugural season was 2001.

PLL stands for Premier Lacrosse League. The league was co-founded in 2018 by former MLL MVP Paul Rabil and his brother,

Michael. In an article on the U.S. Lacrosse Magazine website, Corey McLaughlin wrote, "Players grew frustrated with stagnant wages, low attendance and a questionable media deal that limited viewership." The Rabils met with MLL officials – including former MLL commissioner David Gross – in 2017 to discuss buying the league, but according to McLaughlin's article, Rabil said talks broke down and negotiations never continued when Sandy Brown took over as commissioner in 2018.

In response, the Rabils founded the Premier Lacrosse League and came out of the gate firing. The league had six teams, and unlike traditional sports models, the teams all travel to the same city to play in a two-day event as opposed to each team having its own base city. Over 120 players changed allegiances from MLL to PLL, as they were promised a pay increase (a New York Times article said the average salary was $35,000), health benefits, and equity stakes. The new league struck a television rights deal with NBC before ever playing a game.

A risk this large, leaving an established league going into its 19th season, doesn't happen because everything is progressing smoothly. Major League Lacrosse experienced plenty of gaffes and missteps along the way. In 2011, the league averaged a record 6,417 fans per game. From 2012 to 2018, however, that average decreased every year, bottoming out at 3,619 fans per game in 2018. Fans also lashed out against the league for its media rights deal with Lax Sports Network, which put all MLL games on the streaming site behind a $9.99 per month paywall. An overlap with the National Lacrosse League, the professional box lacrosse league in North America, kept many top players unavailable for several weeks at the beginning of the season. A data breach in August of 2017 exposed personal information – including email addresses, phone numbers, mailing addresses, and social security numbers – of every individual in the MLL Player Pool.

The hits continued to occur after the announcement of the PLL. On April 1 (a very unfortunate date to release bad news), two months prior to the new, later start date of the 2019 season, Major League Lacrosse announced three teams – the Charlotte Hounds, Florida Launch, and Ohio Machine – would not operate during the 2019 season. The reasoning was that league ownership agreed on a strategy limiting one team per owner; Jim Davis owned four teams and chose to operate the Dallas Rattlers instead of Charlotte, Florida, or Ohio. This occurred after the league already conducted its collegiate draft (leaving many players without a team) and announced its schedule (after season tickets were already sold). This was also the second time in league history the league contracted multiple teams, going back to six teams.

Despite the long list of negatives, despite the allure of a new league bustling with excitement and an impressive presence on social media, despite numerous players still needing to work a full-time job outside of lacrosse, many players still chose to play in Major League Lacrosse for the 2019 season. Additionally, even though there seems to be fewer MLL fans than ever before, there are superfans in every city that are passionate about their hometown teams.

The question, then, is when there are plenty of other things each individual could be doing, why do the players, coaches, and fans care so much and remain invested in a league that some say is dead in the water and even more people don't even know it exists?

1.
JUNE 1
NEW YORK AT BOSTON

James Fahey: James Cirrone/Pretty Instant

Massachusetts was the place to be for professional lacrosse on the first day of June. Paul Rabil and company were kicking off the inaugural PLL season at Gillette Stadium – home of the New England Patriots and lacrosse fan/NFL head coach Bill Belichick – in Foxborough, Massachusetts. Twenty-one miles northeast, the Boston Cannons were beginning their 2019 season as well, opening up their new home, Veterans Memorial Stadium in Quincy.

From 2007 to 2018, the Boston Cannons played home games at Harvard Stadium in Allston, Massachusetts, a neighborhood within Boston. The lone exception was 2015, when the Cannons played home games at Gillette Stadium. In March of 2019, the team announced it would invest over $1.5 million in renovations to Veterans Memorial Stadium, including a state-of-the-art digital scoreboard and public address system, new seats in the main stand, a luxury pavilion, new locker rooms, and an upgraded press box.

Two and a half hours before the game, the stadium was already filling up, and the party had already started. Youth teams played games on the turf field. Joshua Tree, a Boston-based U2 cover band, played the hits. There was a rock-climbing wall for kids and a beer garden for adults. Sitting in the newly renovated stands, taking it all in, was Bill O'Brien.

O'Brien clearly stood out among those already in attendance, even without showing off his six-feet-four-inch, 235-pound frame. He wore a red Cannons polo and wore his hair in a braid, signifying the tradition and connection he has to his Native American roots. Like O'Brien, lacrosse originally comes from Native Americans. To the people he is closest to, O'Brien said lacrosse is more like a religion than a sport.

"Lacrosse to the Iroquois is a gift given to them from the Creator," he said. "It's known as the Medicine Game. It's actually a ceremony that's held every spring that is essentially a big lacrosse game. No pads, wooden sticks, and it's played as a form of medicine to heal the community. It's a renewal ceremony. So, when people say lacrosse is more than a sport, it's intertwined in the culture, the history, the heritage of the Iroquois people."

O'Brien, whose father is Onondaga and mother is Irish, was in his first season with MLL, earning a spot on the Cannons practice squad. He started playing in middle school but played football at Sacred Heart University. Playing outside linebacker, O'Brien made 49 tackles, 6.5 tackles for a loss, four sacks, and one interception his senior season.

He worked out with the Buffalo Bills in the summer and tried out for several Canadian Football League teams but was unable to procure a roster spot. He went to work full-time for a health-care company and then help his cousins – including former Tewaaraton Award (NCAA Division 1 lacrosse's award for the most outstanding player) winners Lyle and Miles Thompson – create Thompson Brothers Lacrosse, which holds lacrosse camps and clinics.

His work with Thompson Brothers Lacrosse reignited his passion for the sport, and he earned a tryout with the NLL's New England Black Wolves. He has played in the NLL since 2014.

As a professional athlete, lacrosse has provided O'Brien with a larger platform, and it is not one he takes for granted. In 2016, the Dakota Access Pipeline was approved for construction in the northern United States, including under part of Lake Oahe near Standing Rock Indian Reservation. The Standing Rock Sioux claimed the pipeline would endanger their main source of drinking water and the sacred tribal grounds. The site became a camp for "water protectors" – Native Americans, environmentalists, and activists alike – to demonstrate against the construction of the oil pipeline. Unfortunately, there were instances of violence, making the situation worse. With that in mind, O'Brien, Lyle Thompson, and University of Albany men's lacrosse head coach Scott Marr drove from upstate New York to South Dakota to lend their support and play some lacrosse to provide some medicine.

"We drove from there out to South Dakota with the intention of bringing good medicine, healing people, show them that, 'Hey, look, as professional athletes, we support you, and as just people, we support you and what you're fighting against,'" O'Brien said. "You can do this or that, but by being out there on the front line, showing support, talking to people, figuring out what their concerns are and how you can help, and at the end of the day using lacrosse to inspire, motivate, and reenergize people was pretty cool."

In addition to his philanthropic endeavors, O'Brien is known as quite the personality in the lacrosse community. As he sat in the stands at Veterans Memorial Stadium, Boston's opponent, the New York Lizards, arrived. Lizards attackman Dylan Molloy – who played with O'Brien at training camp for the NLL's Buffalo Bandits – noticed him sitting and yelled, "Thrilla," which is O'Brien's nickname. O'Brien has his own YouTube channel where he uploads videos about fitness, his life, and he even puts a camera on his helmet during local box lacrosse games he plays in in order to show people what the sport is like.

"I like to show people that life is about having a good time," O'Brien said. "While going out to North Dakota and doing philanthropy and giving back is very important, and we do those things, you can use your platform to inspire, to motivate, to give people a perspective they may not have otherwise had."

With the Cannons, O'Brien is getting a perspective he didn't previously have as a player in MLL. While Lyle Thompson is a star player for the Chesapeake Bayhawks, Miles, Jeremy, and Ty Thompson – all left Major League Lacrosse for the PLL. O'Brien acknowledged the PLL provides great opportunities for other players, but he felt MLL was the right opportunity for him. One of the things he was most excited about being in MLL was playing in front of a home-team fan base, particularly the sports-crazy fans in the Boston area.

"It's funny because a lot of about 10 or 12 New England Black Wolves fans heard I was playing for Boston and said, 'We're going to be there game one, so be ready. We're going to get rowdy,'" he said. "I imagine it's going to be an awesome environment to play in. I mean, look at this stadium. They're doing it right out here. Rob Hale – the owner – down to the coaching staff, Coach [Sean] Quirk, and they're doing it right. It's exciting to be here. You can feel it. There's an energy in the air. The fans are buzzing. It's going to be a lot of good lacrosse. They're ready, so we'll be ready."

While the fans may have been ready, the newly renovated sound system wasn't quite as prepared. Kennedy Elsey, co-host of the radio show Karson and Kennedy on Boston radio station Mix 104.1, was slated to sing the National Anthem. As she started singing, her microphone did not work. The fans in attendance were there to help her out, however, and the entire crowd sang the National Anthem in unison.

In that crowd was Cannons season-ticket holder Susan Thibeault and her three children. Even though it wasn't what was supposed to happen, Thibeault said it was one of the best sports moments she's ever witnessed.

"My kids singing along without having to tell them to do it was awesome," she said. "Sometimes, they aren't paying attention, but they were singing along with everybody. It was one of the best sports moments I've ever been a part of. For everyone to come together, that was just incredible."

The Thibeault family got involved in lacrosse around 2014; Susan's son attended a youth league open practice and fell in love with the sport. Her daughters quickly followed suite, but because there was no girls' league, Susan helped form a team. Now, all three children play, she coaches at the youth level, and her husband coaches at the high school level.

Much like how they were introduced to the sport through her son, he also introduced the family to the Cannons. They enrolled him in the team's camp, held at Endicott College, and he received a ticket to a Cannons game as part of the package. She said her kids became obsessed, and they bought season tickets.

"Our youngest was close to [former Cannons goalie] Tyler Fiorito. He actually sent her a game jersey for her birthday," she said. "My youngest was 'Fan of the Game' at Endicott against the Lizards, and the Lizards complained about how loud she was during the game. If you ever need someone to cheer you on, bring Lorelai."

Thibeault said going to Cannons games provides a great sense of community. They have gotten to know other season-ticket holders and have even sat with parents of players like Cannons defender James Fahey and former Boston first-round draft pick Trevor Baptiste.

What she loves the most, however, is the interactions the players have with her kids.

"We go to three or four Red Sox games a year. My husband's been to a Patriots game. We used to have season tickets to the [New England Revolution], but being able to meet the players is a totally different experience," she said. "With soccer, you have to get down to Autograph Alley, and it's a couple minutes. With the Cannons, it's come, hang out, come chill. They give their time to the fans.

"I love it," she added. "[The kids] give their hearts to the sport, and the players give them the love back."

One reason Cannons players have an especially good relationship with their fans is because they were once on the other side of the equation. Several players on the active roster and practice squad grew up in the New England area and went to Cannons games as kids, including Fahey (Boxford, Massachusetts), goalie Nick Marrocco

(Duxbury, Massachusetts), and midfielder Martin Bowes (Quincy, Massachusetts).

"It's pretty cool there's people passionate about the Cannons. Being able to feel that love for the game of lacrosse is pretty special," Marrocco said. "I think having the opportunity to be in our position, playing pro and being able to share that interaction, is something we're going to continue. You know, it's kind of a privilege for us, too."

Before Marrocco, Duxbury was known for another high-level lacrosse player: Max Quinzani. He played his high school lacrosse at Duxbury High School under legendary head coach Chris Sweet, and he helped the school win state championships in 2004, 2005, and 2006; he was named The Boston Globe's Player of the Year in both 2005 and 2006, and he set the national high school record for career points (577), breaking the record previously held by the iconic Casey Powell.

Quinzani played collegiately at Duke University, where he was a three-time USILA All-American selection, broke the program's single-season goals record, and helped Duke win its first national championship in 2010. He was drafted that year by the Boston Cannons with the third overall pick in the MLL Collegiate Draft. In his second season, Quinzani scored the game-winning goal with one-second remaining in the semi-finals of the playoffs, a game known as part of the Hurricane Games (both the semi-final contests and the championship game were played in Annapolis, Maryland while Hurricane Irene hit the mainland). The Cannons would go on to win the franchise's first championship that season.

Marrocco's best friend was one of Quinzani's brothers, and they would go to Cannons games to root on the hometown hero.

"Any access to a city where you actually have a pro lacrosse team is pretty unique," he said. "Coming from a town where the parents dug lacrosse, people in general loved lacrosse, we looked up to the top-notch players, and that was the Cannons."

At Duxbury, Marrocco was a two-time All-America selection. He played collegiately at Georgetown University, where he immediately moved into the starting lineup as a freshman. As a senior, he posted a career-best 7.95 goals against average, was selected as the Most Outstanding Player of the BIG EAST Tournament, and was a First Team USILA All-American selection. He also was heavily involved in lacrosse off-the-field, writing a book, *Lacrosse the Globe*. The book was a project for one of his classes and examined how the sport can grow not just nationally but internationally, with the premise that we could see Japan against Kenya in a future World Lacrosse Championships final. The World Lacrosse Championships were founded in 1967 and are held every four years; in 13 competitions, only two teams – The United States and Canada – have won the tournament, and only one other team – Australia – has even played in the finals.

"It was an entrepreneurship class," Marrocco said about the book. "That teacher was like, 'Alright, you're going to write a book.' Most of the people were like, 'This is ridiculous. I'm dropping this class right away,' but I was like, 'Oh, this is different. I want to try something out of my comfort zone.' He told us we could write about anything we were passionate about. I, obviously, have a passion for lacrosse.

"I wanted to talk about how the game was growing," he added, "so I basically wrote this book about the growth of the sport of lacrosse, where it came from, and using other stories of different sports, like the Jamaican bobsled team, some different stories where you wouldn't think that sport or team to succeed, how they found the path to success, and how that could be put into the sport of lacrosse."

Marrocco went undrafted in the 2018 MLL Collegiate Draft, but the Cannons picked him up from the MLL Player Pool on June 6. Marrocco started the final four games of the season for Boston, who was 3-7 at the time. Marrocco went 2-2 and had the best goals against average (12.56) and save percentage (.547) among the six players that appeared in goal for the Cannons.

He kept his position going into the 2019 season and proved his rookie season was no fluke. Against the Lizards in the season opener, Marrocco made 16 saves to help Boston beat New York, 13-12.

"Nick has been so committed in the offseason," Cannons head coach Sean Quirk said. "He was a guy that had options to play elsewhere. He re-signed with us for a couple years, and he worked so hard, always seeing shots and working out on his own. He's going to be a great goalie."

In front of Marrocco was Fahey. Like Marrocco, Fahey grew up going to Cannons games and hoping to play for them one day. He attended UMass-Amherst, and in 39 career games, he made 15 starts, leading the team in caused turnovers as a senior (20) in 2014. Also like Marrocco, Fahey went undrafted; unlike his goalie, however, Fahey was not picked up as a free agent that season, nor did he make any roster the following year.

It wasn't until 2016 Fahey made an MLL roster; he was added to the Cannons after making the team through an open tryout. After playing in 12 games for Boston his first season, Fahey was traded to Atlanta. Boston reacquired him the following season.

It took Fahey time to earn consistent playing time, but he acknowledged he had an advantage many other young players don't when coming into the league and trying to establish themselves.

"After I graduated college, I had plans to go back to school," he said. "I did have time to dedicate to putting in the work into getting in this league. For a lot of guys, that's kind of the struggle young rookies have. I was fortunate to have a couple years off of work. I had two years from when I graduated college to when I went back to school for higher education. I didn't have to work a nine-to-five job. I didn't have to work 40 hours a week."

Fahey's journey to stick on a roster was a challenge, but he blossomed in 2019, becoming one of the faces of the league. When the league rebranded itself in March of 2019, not only was Fahey's face plastered on several graphics, the league also created several videos promoting some of its individual players and their unique personalities. Fahey represented the Cannons as "The Slasher" with the tag line "It feels good being bad, just ask James Fahey…" He was also named one of Boston's "Most Eligible Singles" by The Improper Bostonian.

His personality has made him not only a leader on the Cannons, but one of the best defenders in the league.

"He brings so much energy and leadership," Quirk said. "Even last night, at our final practice before getting ready for this game, he was a guy that was stepping up and getting guys going. He's an energizer out there."

Fahey said he is humbled by the newfound attention, but that he is happy just to be a part of it all.

"Growing up, I always kind of looked at it as this is a goal, to play professional lacrosse. I didn't really think it was going to come to reality," he said. "My story is I didn't get drafted out of college. I wasn't in the supplemental [draft]. I walked on. It's just that dream of being in Major League Lacrosse, in MLL, it was there. It was a really big priority."

While Marrocco and Fahey are in the early stages of their careers, Martin Bowes has been in the league since 2013. This was his first season back in Boston since 2016. After five games with the Cannons in 2016, he was picked up by the Atlanta Blaze in their inaugural season, and then he played for the Florida Launch for two seasons.

He received a warm welcome back from the Cannons fans. Whenever he stepped on the field against the Lizards, the crowd erupted. It certainly helped that he had a lot of family and friends at the game, since they were playing in his hometown. Playing in the first professional lacrosse game in Quincy was one of Bowes's career highlights.

"I'm honestly having trouble putting it to words," he said. "More than anything, I'm grateful for friends and family that were able to make it out here. I played my high school lacrosse on this field. It's surreal. I always dreamed of playing for the Cannons. I did when we were back at Harvard. I spent a couple years away in Florida. Being able to be back here for the inaugural game is pretty special and humbling, and I'm really grateful."

Because MLL players have jobs outside of playing in the league, whether it's working on Wall Street, teaching, or running their own camps and clinics, teams only practice together once a week, usually the night before the game.

Bowes said having other guys on the team that shared similar experiences with the Cannons growing up helped build some extra chemistry.

"It instantly gives us something to gel," he said. "One of the challenges in this league is building chemistry quickly. We get such little time together. Something like this, to have that emotional connection to other guys in a similar situation, only adds value to the team as a whole."

While Marrocco, Fahey, and Bowes attended Cannons games growing up and dreamed of playing for their hometown team, they aren't the only players on the roster that grew up going to MLL games and wanting to play professional lacrosse.

Attackman Will Sands grew up in Locust Valley, New York. Lacrosse is the family sport. His father, Steven, played lacrosse at Hamilton College and graduated as the program's all-time leading scorer with 156 points. His uncle, Richard, also played at Hamilton while another uncle, Marty, played at Union College.

Sands grew up as a Lizards fan, the same team Boston was opening its 2019 season against. Despite not being their biggest fan anymore, Sands said he sees a lot of similarities between his childhood support of the Lizards and the love the Cannons fans have for their team.

"It's the best part of the league, and it's the best part about being in Boston. The fans here are really passionate about the Cannons, and they're passionate about the players," he said. "I know that used to be me a while back when I was going to the MLL games in Long Island, and I know how much it meant to me when the players gave me attention, so I know us as players, you try to do a good job of giving back. At the end of the day, it's all to keep this amazing sport going, and we want to give back as much as we possibly can."

Sands was a three-sport athlete at the Friends Academy, playing lacrosse, soccer, and basketball. He made the varsity lacrosse team as an eighth-grader and, eventually, broke the school's all-time scoring record (327 points). He was No. 49 on the *Inside Lacrosse* top-100 recruit rankings and chose to continue his lacrosse career at Bucknell University.

At Bucknell, he hit the ground running, starting all 15 games as a freshman and finishing second on the team in points. He would go on to become a three-time All-Patriot League selection and earn USILA Third Team All-American honors. He became just the third Bison to reach 200 career points and graduated with school records in career assists (141) and assists in a single season (55).

Sands was selected with the first pick in the third round of the 2018 MLL Collegiate Draft (No. 19 overall), and again, he made an immediate impact. In each of his first two contests, he totaled five points on three goals and two assists. He appeared in five games total as a rookie, scoring seven goals and adding 10 assists, even earning a selection to the MLL All-Star Game. Unfortunately, in the second half of a June 23 game against the Lizards, Sands took a slash across the hand, suffered a broken hand, and was forced to miss the rest of the season.

He wasn't happy that his rookie year was cut short, but it was a positive experience that had him wanting to come back for more.

"I had so much fun playing with these guys and playing for Boston and for the fans of Boston," he said. "I thought it was a first-class organization, so it was a no brainer for me to decide to come back."

In his first game back, Sands was rather quiet. He tallied one assist, but the Cannons initiated most of their offense from the midfield position instead of sending it behind the goal to Sands.

Quirk said for the first game, the team was just happy to have Sands back on the field and getting comfortable again.

"He's our quarterback back there," the Cannons head coach said. "Just to get him back in it, he hasn't played this competitively since his injury last year. I think this game gave him a lot of confidence, getting a big W. He played well, and he's just going to keep getting better."

The first week of the season is an exciting time of year. Fans welcome getting to see the top players in the sport compete and create highlights, and every team – no matter the record the year prior – has a chance to compete for a championship.

The beginning of the 2019 season, however, also brought some extra skepticism from outside observers. With the advent of the PLL, "fans" were more than happy to share their criticisms of MLL on social media. Glorified beer league was a phrase frequently used. Many observers also prognosticated the death of the league. It was an extra point of contention as the leagues opened their seasons in relatively close proximity.

The players saw those comments, and they did not appreciate them. They did, however, quickly point out just how wrong they thought those gloom and doom reactions were.

"I love the MLL. I love playing in the MLL," Sands said. "I chose to play in the MLL for a reason. I was fortunate to have a choice to play between the two leagues. I picked the MLL for a reason. I think it really has a great community, especially here in Boston. I enjoy playing lacrosse for that sort of community, not as much for traveling and showcasing. I have respect for the people who started the new league. I'm not against it. I'm not rooting against them. I'm just here to play lacrosse and enjoy it. I found doing that in Boston and in the MLL was the best way for me to personally accomplish that."

Players like Fahey, who scratched and clawed in order to make a roster, also see it as an opportunity.

It was reminiscent of the landscape of professional wrestling in the mid-1990s. The World Wrestling Federation was the prominent sports entertainment organization with the biggest shows and the best talent until Ted Turner took over World Championship Wrestling and decided it wanted to rival WWF, which was experiencing a lull in popularity. WCW took some of WWF's best superstars, including eventual Hall of Famers Hulk Hogan, Razor Ramon, and Diesel. With a hole at the top of the card, new superstars were able to shine in the main event, including legendary figures such as Brett Hart, Shawn Michaels, and Stone Cold Steve Austin.

For MLL in 2019, top players like Rabil, Kyle Harrison, Tom Schreiber, and Jordan Wolf – who had dominated the league for many years – were gone. The league wouldn't be better because those players were gone, but Fahey was confident a new crop of younger talent was more than ready to step up and make a name for themselves.

"Last year, when the world games were playing and the main guys from every team were playing overseas in Israel for Team USA, that created that vacuum you see now in the league. All the big-name players were gone," Fahey said. "It was just guys on the practice squad, guys who didn't necessarily have that big name, guys who didn't necessarily get their shot. They had their shot that weekend. We coincidentally played New York that weekend and when I tell you, you take all those big names and you take, I won't necessarily say egos, but you take the allure out of player names in those games, we still had 60 minutes of great product of lacrosse. After that game, I know a lot of guys, myself personally, we all had in our heads if this other league happens, we're going to be good.

"There's a lot of young guys, especially college guys who didn't get drafted right away, guys that are taking this very seriously," he added, "that you're going to know their name by the end of the year."

If, according to random people on Twitter, 2019 was going to be the beginning of the end for Major League Lacrosse, it was not evident in Quincy on June 1.

The Cannons played their first game in their new home in front of a sold-out crowd of 5,025 people. Not only did the fans show up, they showed up early and there was a buzz and energy throughout the game, even after when players were on the field signing autographs and taking pictures.

"It was definitely louder than I remember anywhere else," Bowes said. "It can be electric in here. We're not going to be selling out 50,000-seat arenas. I think six, seven thousand is something, a mark we can hit regularly. The people that came today, I think they're going to come back. I think they had a really good experience because it was more electric and more intimate."

Boston left its fans happy, securing the victory, and Sands said their energy was vital to the team's success.

"They make you feel like you're playing at home and playing for someone other than yourself, and you're playing for the community here," he said. "That's what's special. When you're playing professional sports, or sports in general, when you feel like you're playing for something other than yourself and something bigger than yourself, it's usually when you get the best athleticism on the field. People really fly around when it's not about them, when it's about something a little bigger."

The Cannons players were not only happy with the win; they were happy their lacrosse journeys and choice to stick with Major League Lacrosse, even through down times, had led them to this experience.

Boston midfielder Kyle Denhoff, a 2013 undrafted free agent from Division 3 St. John Fisher College who climbed the ranks in MLL to become a multiple-time all-star, took in the moment.

"It's been a ride," he said. "Going to play D3 because I was hurt in high school, and then Coach [Tim] Soudan gave me a look in Rochester and ended up making my first game ever. I remember going into that camp and looking around at the guys I was playing with. [Former MLL All-Star] Kevin Leveille is on the field. [former Tewaaraton Award winner and Team USA player] Mike Leveille is on the field. [Hall of Famer] Mark Millon is on the field. I'm like, 'No way.' I just wanted to make the practice squad. To turn it into seven years, packed house, at a brand-new stadium, I'm lucky. I'm lucky for sure."

2.
JUNE 21
DALLAS AT ATLANTA

Tommy Palasek: Brett Davis/Pretty Instant

Henry Grady High School is located in Atlanta, Georgia, adjacent to the historic Piedmont Park. It also is the home for a number of memorable pieces of pop culture. Its alumni include Chick-fil-A founder S. Truett Cathy (who graduated from the school when it was previously named Boys High), Martin Luther King Jr.'s daughter Yolanda King, actor Eric Roberts, five former professional baseball players, and two former professional football players.

The high school was used to fill in for the famous T.C. Williams High School during filming for the movie *Remember the Titans* and was also where Peter Parker went to school in *Spider-Man: Homecoming.* The movies *The Duff* and *Ride Along* (starring Ice Cube and Kevin Hart) also filmed scenes at Grady High School.

In 2019, it was also home to Major League Lacrosse's Atlanta Blaze. The team moved from Fifth Third Bank in the suburbs of Kennesaw, Georgia to the high school partially hoping to attract the foot traffic of Piedmont Park and Midtown (due to maintenance at Grady Stadium in August, the Blaze played their final three home games just outside of Atlanta at Silverbacks Stadium, home of the former Atlanta Silverbacks soccer team and Atlanta Renegades Rugby Football Club).

Two and a half hours before the Blaze game against the Dallas Rattlers did not have the same block party feel as in Quincy earlier in the month; it actually was quite quiet with only a few staff members even there. There was one early fan, however: Brett Stevens.

Stevens showed up early to help the team's staff set up and get ready for the evening's game.

"When I'm with my friends, and we're watching the game, we have so much fun," he said. "What I want to do is, I always tell people, 'Bring me a solution. How can I help? What can I do?' That's the part of me saying, 'What can I do to help?' because I enjoy coming here so much and hanging out with my friends watching great lacrosse. I'm one of those bring me a solution, so the least I can do is bring you some manpower."

Stevens grew up as a big football and baseball fan. He first saw lacrosse in 2007 and urged his son to try it out. As father and son enjoyed their entry into the sport, they looked for the game at the highest level. They became fans of the Charlotte Hounds since it was the closest team to them, and once a year, they'd make the four-hour trip to Charlotte to see a Hounds game.

In August of 2015, Major League Lacrosse announced a new

expansion team in Atlanta to begin play in the 2016 season. Stevens instantly became a fan.

"I was probably the first season ticket holder. I immediately bought season tickets," he said. "We'd all tailgate. We'd watch the game. The players, I'm a big Randy Staats fan. I love watching the guy play. He's fantastic. Mark Matthews was here for a while. I'm a big Mark Matthews fan. Just the quality of play and the accessibility of the players is what I like. They always took time for the fans. They made the fans feel important. They could not take enough pictures. They couldn't spend enough time. They really brought people in, which I thought was important. I think they always felt the Blaze appreciated their fans, which was so refreshing for pro sports."

Stevens appreciated the connection the fans made with the players and the support the franchise gave to the community. He's seen its benefits first-hand. Stevens was a Marine for four years, and now he runs the Atlanta chapter of Shootout for Soldiers.

Shootout for Soldiers is a 24-hour event featuring 24 one-hour lacrosse games. The event acts as a fundraiser for the Wounded Warrior Project, and according to the company's website, the purpose is to educate the community about the challenges veterans face when coming home, bring the civilian and military communities together, and help other non-profits.

The first year the event took place in Atlanta was 2016. Stevens said since they started, the Atlanta event has raised nearly $200 million, and that they raised $45,000 in 2019.

It's an event he holds dear to his heart, and he said the Blaze had been especially supportive.

"[Blaze GM] Spencer Ford and [Blaze head coach] Liam Banks, they came out to the Shootout for Soldiers event. They coached the veterans' game," he said. "They were out there with us, shaking hands with players. It meant a lot to our event. It meant a lot to the veterans to see MLL coaches out there. They spent time shaking hands, having fun with it, and then afterwards, did some interviews and took some pictures. By them doing that, they came up, broke the training schedule, coached a game, and came back. They showed, 'We care about the community as well.' In turn, we need to be out there supporting them. They have supported us when we've asked them to help us."

Stevens said it would be the relationship between the community and the league, its teams, and its players that helps it survive and grow.

"They come out here, the guys will stop and sign an autograph, sign a shirt, whatever you need, shake hands," he said. "I remember players saying, 'Thanks for coming out.' Thanks for coming out. They spent so much time taking pictures, whatever we needed. I found that refreshing. As a parent, you're paying money for the family to go out, and when I was at some of the other pro sports, they don't even acknowledge you, not even a head nod. It was just another day. They were very distant where the Blaze brought people in and had that 'we are family' type of feel. We're happy you're here."

Stevens said attackman Randy Staats was one of his favorite Blaze players. Unfortunately for Stevens, he hadn't had too many opportunities to see Staats play in Major League Lacrosse, let alone with the Atlanta Blaze.

Staats – a native of Six Nations, Ontario – was drafted out of Syracuse in the fourth round of the 2015 MLL Collegiate Draft by the Rochester Rattlers (who moved to Dallas for the 2018 season). He played five games his rookie season and was traded to the Blaze the following year. In two seasons in his first stint with Atlanta, Staats played 18 of 28 games. He was traded back to Dallas the following season, and he played in only two games in 2018. From 2016 to 2018, he missed time due to the overlap between the MLL and NLL seasons. In the NLL, Staats plays for the Georgia Swarm, where he won the 2016 NLL Rookie of the Year and helped the Swarm win the league championship in 2017.

In October of 2018, Major League Lacrosse announced the 2019 season would begin on May 31; this was the same day as the third and final game of the 2019 NLL Finals, essentially removing the overlap between the two leagues. Most box players, including Staats and Georgia Swarm and Atlanta Blaze teammates Shayne Jackson and Bryan Cole, were available for MLL training camp for the first time.

Being with the team at training camp as opposed to coming in midway through the season made a huge difference for the players; they had a better opportunity to make the roster, and they developed chemistry sooner.

"Spencer asked if I wanted to play. I wanted to play still. I hadn't played field too often the past few years, and I wanted to give it a shot,"

Jackson said. "They had an opportunity with the other league starting, and I jumped on it."

Staats played box lacrosse growing up in Six Nations. When the Toronto Nationals – the first Canadian MLL team – moved to Hamilton, Staats was exposed to the prospects of playing field lacrosse professionally as well as getting to watch one of the best players to play both box and field lacrosse, John Grant Jr., live and in person.

"He's one of my favorite players to watch and one of the best players to play the game," Staats said. "He's a special player, special person. He's just really good. He does things that people don't think of doing in certain situations, like, say, running down the wrong side and throwing a reverse backhand bottom corner or throwing a fake backhand and then rolling it between his legs. That's something you don't get every day. It was special to watch, and it's still special to watch."

Grant Jr. originally retired from MLL after the 2016 season; in his final regular season game, he scored 10 goals against the New York Lizards, setting a single-game record. He came out of retirement days before the start of the 2019 season to play with the Denver Outlaws, the team he was coaching and the team he played three seasons with and helped win its first MLL championship.

During his return, Grant Jr. broke the league's all-time scoring record – a mark that was originally his but broken by Paul Rabil in 2018 – in the team's third game of the season, which occurred in Atlanta with Staats on the field.

Staats said it was still an honor to be out there and see him do it, even if it was against him and his team, and he lost the game. Just like how Grant Jr. inspired Staats to become a professional, Staats and Jackson are doing the same thing, especially in Atlanta, not known as a hotbed of lacrosse. Staats and Jackson not only star for the Blaze (the two combined for five goals and 10 total points in the team's 13-11 victory over Dallas on June 21), they also both star for the city's NLL franchise, the Georgia Swarm.

Both Jackson and Staats are proud and humbled to make even the smallest impact on the lacrosse community in Atlanta.

"They're lucky to have some of the best lacrosse players in the world play right in their backyard," Jackson said. "I have been helping a lot with the youth out here, coaching, and the kids always come up and say how they love coming to the games and watching, and, hopefully, if we can have a kid want to play in the pros someday, he can look up to the guys that are playing and maybe he reaches his goals and go to college."

"It's crazy to see," Staats added. "When I first started here for indoor, we didn't get that many fans, and then it took four years, but we have a decent fanbase. It's definitely growing. I see it growing. I see all the little kids coming here. When we were up in Kennesaw, there was a good fan base there. I think introducing the game to new people and allowing their children or young adults watch and see what we can do and see this is something they can pursue later on. Now, maybe this can be their goal one day. It's pretty cool to be that role model in both leagues for this area."

Staats transferred to Syracuse after playing two years at Onondaga Community College. In his freshman year at Onondaga, another two-year transfer was playing his senior season at Syracuse: Tommy Palasek.

Palasek – who went to Johns Hopkins in 2009 and 2010 – shined at Syracuse, totaling 54 points on 24 goals and 30 assists in his senior season. His success at Syracuse may have seemed sudden to some, but Palasek put years of work into it. He started playing lacrosse at five-years-old; his father, Tom, had played two years of JV lacrosse at Syracuse. Tommy was one of seven children growing up in Rocky Point, New York, and he said that without cell phones, he had no choice but to spend most of his time outside playing all types of sports including lacrosse; his family even had a net in the backyard.

He remembered that without YouTube or much lacrosse on television, he was forced to travel to find lacrosse games. When playing in tournaments in Maryland, he would go to local high school games. He also made sure to go plenty of New York Saints (a former NLL team that became inactive in 2003 after 15 seasons) and New York Lizards games. Playing professional lacrosse was always his dream, and his connection to the MLL players at the time inspired him.

"I was a huge Powell fan," Palasek said, referring to the iconic trio of lacrosse playing brothers: Casey, Ryan, and Mike. "I remember watching Mikey play against the All-Stars. It was Team USA and him and his brothers were playing on the same line. I can remember that like it was yesterday, how incredible it was. I had three brothers, too.

It was cool to see a family that grew up in upstate New York and made it to that level."

After his successful senior season, Palasek was selected in the fourth round of the 2012 MLL Collegiate Draft by his hometown New York Lizards. New York, at the time, was in turmoil. The team won just five games the previous summer, it was undergoing ownership and coaching changes, and many star players positioned themselves to get traded to another team.

Without stars like Grant Jr., Tim Goettelmann, and Matt Danowski (the team's leading scorer in 2011) on attack, there were plenty of opportunities for Palasek to play his way into the lineup. As a rookie, he played 11 games, finishing fifth on the team in scoring with 26 points. The Lizards surprisingly made the playoffs. Over the next four seasons in New York, Palasek averaged 28.75 points per season, yet his role lessened over the years; the Lizards brought in MLL All-Stars like Rob Pannell, Paul Rabil, Ned Crotty, and Will Manny. In 2017, Palasek appeared in only 11 of the team's 14 games, his lowest total since his rookie season.

In February of 2016, MLL instituted a new player movement policy, similar to free agency in other leagues. Players that had at least five years of experience and an expiring contract could move to any team they chose, provided the new team sent the former team a draft pick for compensation. Palasek's contract expired after the 2017 season, and with the player movement policy, he was convinced by then-Atlanta head coach Dave Huntley and then-Atlanta assistant coach Spencer Ford to join the Blaze.

Palasek played 13 games in his first season in Atlanta and finished fourth on the team with 26 points. While he embraced his new role as a leader with Atlanta, he was grateful for the time he spent fighting to see playing time in New York.

"That time in my life helped me to be a more complete player now," he said. "My whole life, I was a dodger. I could get to the cage no problem but not really an outside shooter, not moving off ball. I didn't need to. … At Syracuse, the ball was in my stick 15 times a game. In high school, the ball is in my stick 25 times a game. I had 100 assists in my senior season of high school. Then [with the Lizards] Rob [Pannell] and Ned Crotty come in. Paul Rabil comes in. The next thing you know, if I don't learn how to play off ball or do the other things, I'm standing on the sidelines watching."

Palasek said one of the biggest challenges for players in Major League Lacrosse is pushing themselves when they're away from the team and no one, like a coach, is in front of them holding them accountable. He said a big reason why many players don't last long in the league is because when they get further and further away from college, where they had a workout routine, it can be tougher to stay on top of their development in the offseason.

He wishes that outside observers would give the MLL players the respect he feels they deserve for the work that goes into the responsibility of being a professional athlete without the million-dollar contracts.

"There's a lot that goes into that," he said. "So many other pro sports, they get paid to wake up, maybe help promote or do something for the team, but their main objective is to get two hours of workouts in, stretch, eat well, do all the things that make you the best player you can be, but they get paid to do it during the week. Us, we're not getting paid to do it during the week. We're getting paid to come here, show up, and be good enough to do it on the weekends."

Still, Palasek, who works at a high school during the off-season, is not one to complain about his situation. He said he is more than happy to put the work in. Big salary or not, he just enjoys what he does.

"I love playing so much," he said. "I really like the city of Atlanta. I love the idea of having a home stadium. I love the idea of building something new here."

Now, in Atlanta, Palasek is the veteran star who teammates look up to.

"Palasek is one of the most quiet producers in the league," said Blaze goalie Chris Madalon. "You didn't always hear of his name on a star-studded lineup in New York, but I'm happy he's becoming a face of the franchise in Atlanta, and he's a great player

"You can put him anywhere on the field," Madalon added, "and he's going to be a great teammate and get the job done."

In addition to Palasek, Madalon was another former Lizard that moved to the Blaze in 2018. While Palasek didn't always shine over his All-Star counterparts, Madalon was completely blocked from playing time.

Madalon was on the Lizards from 2014 through 2017, but in four seasons he played in only one game for 30 minutes. He was behind Drew Adams, who played 10 years for New York from 2009 through

2018, was a five-time All-Star, was named Goalie of the Year three times, and helped the team win the league championship in 2015.

It would've been easy for Madalon to leave MLL, to not have to sacrifice his weekends to sit the bench, but it was important for him to stick with it.

"Just to have the opportunity to play at the next level post-college and continue to be a part of a team, the locker room, is the most exciting part," he said. "In addition to that, just doing it for the fans and the kids in the next generation, I think, is what it's all about.

"Playing goalie at this level is a major challenge," he added. "I think it's something I love doing. It's tough to give up at this point."

Like Palasek, Madalon said the time on the sidelines helped him learn how to be a good teammate, and he forged a strong friendship with Adams, even working camps together.

Madalon joined the Blaze for the 2018 season and was again supposed to be the backup, this time to Adam Ghitelman. Unlike Adams, however, Ghitelman – a college coach – had conflicts that forced him to miss several games at the start of the 2018 season, opening a door for Madalon.

He played in eight games in 2018, going 3-2 and posting a .559 save percentage. When Ghitelman left MLL for the PLL for the 2019 season, the Blaze were confident with Madalon as the team's top goalie.

"Mads is a great, very vocal goalie. He knows exactly what he wants," Blaze defender and captain Liam Byrnes said. "He watches a lot of film. When we do that conference call, he's a big part in that. [Defensive coordinator] Tod [Francis] will go through what he wants to do, and then he'll give it over to Mads. Mads is like, 'This is what we're going to do similar to that,' where he wants to see shots from. He's been great. He's a guy that's been in the league a lot of years."

"I'm really proud of him, watching him, because that position is so hard," Palasek added. "There's plenty of backups who aren't really ready to do it. He's been waiting for his chance. I'm proud of him."

In the game against Dallas, Madalon proved he earned the starting goalie position.

The Atlanta defense was constantly under attack; Dallas players took 63 shots, 31 of which were on cage. Madalon made 20 saves on the night, prompting Rattlers attackman Bryce Wasserman (who had one goal on 10 shots) to say, "He played a special game. He was all over the ball. He was seeing it well. Sometimes, that's how the ball goes. You just have to tip your cap to him, and, hopefully, we get him next time."

Madalon said his journey from longtime backup to starter helps motivate him.

"I think it continues to put a chip on my shoulder to prove that I have the ability to play in this league and am just grateful for any opportunity to play," he said. "It's top 12 goalies in the league at this point on an MLL roster. It's not an easy position to make it this far, and just having the opportunity and continuing to have it for the last seven years now, it's been a ride. It's been a challenge, but I'm excited for where it's gotten me to now."

The men responsible for putting together this Blaze team are general manager Spencer Ford and head coach Liam Banks, both of whom are MLL alumni.

Banks played six seasons in the league with four teams that eventually folded: the Philadelphia Barrage (which the league brought back for the 2020 season), New Jersey Pride, San Francisco Dragons, and Chicago Machine. He moved to Atlanta after his playing career and founded LB3 Lacrosse, a club program in Georgia. Active in the Georgia lacrosse community, Banks was the promoter of the first MLL game in Atlanta when the Rochester Rattlers took on the Boston Cannons. Previously, the league routinely used all-star games and championship games to test prospective cities for future expansion teams. The contest between the Rattlers and Cannons, held on Friday, June 7, 2013, brought 4,417 fans to Fifth Third Bank Stadium. League officials were so pleased with the event, they decided to hold the MLL Championship Game in both 2014 and 2015 in Atlanta before awarding the city its expansion team for 2016; Banks also helped put together those championship games.

Banks said bringing elite lacrosse – both professional and collegiate – to Atlanta was key to help it grow in the region.

"I knew the Greater Atlanta area was never going to be able to grow at the rate I thought it should grow at if we didn't bring down big time lacrosse," he said. "Whether it was NCAA, whether it was the professional games, I thought being a part of this community, I owed to the connections I had to try and get the best lacrosse here.

Ultimately, I never knew it would bring Major League Lacrosse, but we have Major League Lacrosse right now, and kids have the opportunity to watch the best players in the world and emulate what they do and ultimately move on. When you look at the kids going to college from Atlanta, and you look at the timeline there, a lot of them fell under that timeline of seeing their first, whether it was an NCAA game or Major League Lacrosse game here, and now a lot of those kids are moving on to play in college."

Ford was invited to the first league combine and was on the sidelines for the first MLL game in history when his Baltimore Bayhawks defeated the Long Island Lizards, 16-13. He played eight seasons in Major League Lacrosse, including an incredible 2007 season where he played in his first All-Star Game, broke the record for assists in a season (a record that was still standing coming into the 2019 season), and won the Most Improved Player award.

For Ford, MLL isn't just a hobby or a career; it's his life.

"[I] was there to see the energy in the first MLL game. The first goal, the first check, first everything. It has stuck with me," he said. "I'm 43 now. It's been in my life for almost half of my life. It's very, very close to my heart. I've been lucky enough to play and excel on the field, and then I've been lucky enough to be hired with two great organizations with Chesapeake as well as Atlanta. Won some championships and was able to meet a heck of a lot of amazing people. As far as passion, this is my family. This is part of who I am and what I'm all about."

Ford and Banks both say it is a treat to be a part of the league and see its growth and change from when they played in it.

"Everything we did was based on growing lacrosse. Whether it was when I was in New Jersey or out in San Francisco, there was a real emphasis on giving back," Banks said. "The [postgame autograph] signing to this day MLL players still do, so I think when I was playing there was a compete factor, but more of it, for us in our generation, was about growing the game and providing opportunities for the next generation of lacrosse players."

Because they are so invested in the league, because they care so much about the players, coaches, and staff involved, they take the negativity aimed at Major League Lacrosse very personally.

"I commend Major League Lacrosse. It's been in business almost 20 years. As we all know, selling lacrosse isn't an easy thing to do.

Major League Lacrosse has sustained themselves for almost 20 years now," Banks said. "We've got a lot of passionate people involved, in particular our owner, and the league has made some great strides in the last two years, and [MLL commissioner] Sandy Brown has done a nice job of providing Major League Lacrosse players better salaries, has worked harder to improve the league and made a lot of positive changes.

"For me, I think living in the negative energy space on social media can only bring you down. I also think social media is a place where people can present something that may not really be there; it's more of a skeleton of what it is," he added. "I think Major League Lacrosse is going to be around for another 50 years. We now have 12 professional teams in a sense [including PLL teams], so there's more opportunities for players, which is a good thing. Lacrosse is in the spotlight. The infighting, I think myself and all players could do without. It gets a little disrespectful to the talent level of our Major League Lacrosse players."

Ford said the comments on social media are not only upsetting but that the posters are also forgetting how close the lacrosse community is and how the sport is supposed to bring people together, not divide people.

"It hurts. It's a tremendous amount of hurt and pain," he said. "The worst part is I know all these guys. I know they still care about me. I know they still care about this league. You know what, the players did what they thought they had to do. Right, wrong, or indifferent, that's not for me to tell them; that's for them to figure out. Kudos to them for having the faith in each other to do this. We've seen them play a few games. It's very high-level lacrosse.

"There's a lot of strangers that love the game, and that's great they love the game, but they don't know how all of us feel about each other," he added. "To me, they forgot about that one common bond we all have. Lacrosse is a small fraternity. I don't care which league you play in, which school you went to, we look out for one another. I know if I was hurting, and I ran into [former MLL All-Star and current PLL All-Star] Kyle Harrison, he would help me, and he would be there for me the same way I would be there for him. I think that's what's left behind. Money, league, this, that, what they did, what we did, all the talk to me is a bunch of BS. The bottom line is everybody cares about one another. I think, hopefully, one day you'll see everybody back together."

In December of 2017, the lacrosse community at large suffered a tough loss when Atlanta Blaze head coach Dave Huntley unexpectedly passed away. He was a member of the Canadian and National Lacrosse Halls of Fame, and he spent eight seasons coaching in Major League Lacrosse. He helped the Toronto Nationals win the championship in 2009, and at his last stop in Atlanta, he helped stabilize, guide, and grow a new team. He helped the team improve from 4-10 in its inaugural season (Huntley took over for John Tucker after the team's 10th game) to 6-8 the following year. The team was expected to continue to improve the next season.

In his honor, the league created the David Huntley Man of the Year Award, given to a player who demonstrates great sportsmanship, professionalism, and community service. Each team selects a representative, and a panel of voters (including the author of this book) selects a winner. The winner of the inaugural award in 2018 was former Blaze long-stick midfielder and Atlanta-native Scott Ratliff.

In Ratliff's acceptance speech, with teary eyes, he shared his opinion on the greatness Huntley brought to the sport.

"Coach Huntley, everything he did for me as a coach, the biggest thing that stood out to me was the impact he made on me off the field, the interest he took in me off the field, and not just me but every player," he said. "I don't think there's maybe anybody in the history of our sport that made an impact on indoor lacrosse, outdoor lacrosse, Canadian lacrosse, American lacrosse, in the way Coach Huntley did. It's an absolute honor to receive this award."

Huntley was one of Ford's closest friends in the sport. He said Huntley was a big reason the Blaze were able to sign Tommy Palasek. The team brought back Shayne Jackson and Randy Staats, who were a part of that original team in 2016. Part of Ford's goal in building the Blaze roster was to honor the memory of Huntley and help finish the job he started.

"I'll never forget being able to coach with my best friend, Dave Huntley," Ford said. "To work with him and be with him for three years was absolutely amazing. I do know if he was still here today, we'd still be doing this thing together. It's been a really fun ride. There's been a lot of great memories."

3.
JULY 4
CHESAPEAKE AT DENVER

JoJo War Drummer: Ron Chenoy/Pretty Instant

Mile High Fourth of July is the biggest MLL game of the season, in terms of attendance. The game features a postgame fireworks show produced by Zambelli Fireworks where more than 10,000 pyrotechnics are launched not only off the top of the stadium but off the field as well. The fireworks go along with a video tribute played on the stadium's 220-foot-long by 40-foot-high video board.

At least 20,000 fans have attended the game each year since 2008, and it drew 30,000 fans on three different occasions, including a record 31,664 people in 2015.

"It's so cool. Last weekend, we had a good amount of fans out, but what I love is the people who come out are really invested and into it," Outlaws midfielder Mikie Schlosser said. "Fourth of Julys are really special here. Last year was an incredible experience. It was pretty awesome. I'm looking forward to doing it again tonight."

Boston Cannons goaltender Nick Marrocco made his MLL debut when the Cannons took on the Outlaws in the 2018 version of the Mile High Fourth of July game.

"There was something like 30,000 people there," he said. "It was quite the awakening for me just to be in the pro circuit and understand what it's like to have fans care about you as a player and your team."

The fans are treated not only to a great show, but their hometown lacrosse team usually gives plenty of reasons to cheer as well; going into 2019, the Outlaws were 9-4 in Fourth of July contests.

It's a game Outlaws rookie midfielder Zach Runberg, from Centennial, Colorado, remembers going to as a kid and was even more excited to play in for the first time.

Five days prior to the Mile High Fourth of July game, Runberg – who graduated from the University of Denver and made the Outlaws through an open tryout – played in his second career MLL game; it was at Boston in a battle between the two teams at the top of the standings.

It was a high-scoring affair, and Boston made a late run to draw the teams even. They used a 5-1 run in the fourth quarter to tie the game at 16 with 42 seconds remaining. It was time for the rookie to play the hero.

Runberg picked up the ground ball on the ensuing face-off, ran down the field on a fast break, and scored with 20 seconds remaining. Not only was the goal the eventual game-winner, it was also Runberg's first professional goal.

"It was surreal," he said. "I still don't think it has hit me yet. Being able to be in that position and have that opportunity, I'm very grateful for that. I was fortunate enough to be able to put the ball in the back of the net, but I'm thankful for my teammates because if it wasn't for them, I wouldn't be in that position."

Going to Outlaws games as a young lacrosse player, Runberg dreamed of playing professional lacrosse but never thought it was a possibility until his senior year of college. Even then, Runberg wasn't expecting to be drafted; he just knew the Outlaws held open tryouts and figured he might as well show up.

Luckily for Runberg, he impressed.

"Just playing high school lacrosse here," he said, "and then college at DU and now being able to play for the Outlaws is something I really am thankful for.

"I think I'm just lucky enough to wear Outlaws across my chest and be able to play for this organization," he added. "I'm just thankful tryouts went well, and here I am."

Runberg is one of many diamonds in the rough the Denver organization has unearthed over the years. Of the players that helped the Outlaws win the 2018 MLL championship, two were sixth-round draft picks (out of seven rounds), two were seventh-round draft picks, and four were selected in the supplemental draft; in the supplemental draft, players who are not part of a 23-man protected roster are available to be selected by other teams, slightly similar to the Rule 5 Draft in Major League Baseball.

Jon Cohen was promoted to Denver's general manager and director of player personnel prior to the 2019 season. He originally joined the Outlaws staff in 2007 working as the visiting team liaison. He was the team's equipment manager from 2008 through 2010 and was the assistant general manager and assistant coach from 2011 through 2018.

According to head coach Tony Seaman – who was the team's previous general manager – Cohen deserves a lot of credit for finding those late-round steals.

"Jon Cohen is an amazing mind about lacrosse players and their availability and what they're doing. He's a dictionary," he said. "I can just call him and say, 'Man, I saw this kid from Bentley. I know the family a little bit. He's been a wonderful face-off kid up there although they haven't been very successful as a team,' and he goes 'Oh yeah, you mean [Max] Adler?' I say, 'Yeah, that's exactly who I mean.' So, he and

I work so well together. It's been seven years now, and I think we're on the same page, the two of us."

Finding those underrated players is something Cohen takes a lot of pride in. He said he and Seaman have a whiteboard with a hundred names on it of players in college or professional that they need to watch film on and evaluate. It's a skill he's worked on since joining the Outlaws organization, and one that was at an all-time high priority with the advent of the PLL.

"We've always drafted at the end of the rounds because, thank goodness, we're in the championship or win the championship, so we don't get the luxury of having the first overall pick or even in the second round, the tenth pick or seventh pick or however many teams there are," he said. "You have to learn how to find guys that want to play. That's been the most important thing. This new locker room we have is guys that want a shot and deserve a shot for us. That's been the most exciting part, dealing with a bunch of guys that are really fired up to break into pro lacrosse."

One player in particular that put a lot of effort to break into Major League Lacrosse and the Denver Outlaws was goalie Kai Iwamoto, the first player from Japan to appear in an MLL game.

Iwamoto is from Tokyo, Japan and wasn't introduced to the sport until he attended Keio High School, which had a boys' lacrosse program.

"Some of my friends from middle school, they asked me to go to the practice. I went there, tossed the ball, and that's it. I got into it," he said. "Some good players showed their great stick skills to us. I was like, 'That's so sick.' I practiced on the field with varsity with a sophomore or junior's stick, and I made it once behind the back or something. It was a perfect pass, and I was like, 'Oh my God. This is sick. I'm going to play this one.' I went to a lacrosse shop in Japan and bought all the stuff there on the same day."

Iwamoto played club lacrosse in Japan while working. He considered taking over his father's business, but he said his dad told him he needed to study English.

He figured there was no better way to learn the language than go to the country, so at 29-years-old, he moved to Portland, Oregon.

"It's closer to Japan," he said, "and I heard the coffee and beer and food is good."

Iwamoto enrolled at the University of California Irvine to study

English and business and to play lacrosse.

"I wanted to play lacrosse because I love lacrosse," he said. "People who play lacrosse are always awesome to me, always nice to me. Playing lacrosse is a great tool to make American friends, to improve my English skills."

In eight games for UC Irvine in 2017, he posted a .658 save percentage.

Like many other players exiting college, Iwamoto thought he would give professional lacrosse a try. His club team was not heavily recruited, however, so the usual pathway through the Collegiate Draft wasn't an option.

It didn't deter Iwamoto, however. He was more than willing to go to open tryouts.

"There had been no goalie coaches to me. I just played and watched others play or American professionals play or college players play on YouTube, and I analyzed it myself and figured out what they were doing and kept myself improved," he said. "I just wanted professional coaches' advice here. Then, I tried out for the Outlaws for the first time in 2016 and other teams, Boston Cannons or Bayhawks, and I thought I played well, but I didn't make the roster, so I asked the coaches if they had any evaluations for me, and they were like, 'You played very well,' but I was like, 'I think I need to do something different.'"

Iwamoto tried out again for the Denver Outlaws in 2017 and was invited to training camp, but he once again did not make the team. Each year he tried out, he made more connections and friends. After the 2017 tryouts, he worked out with then-Outlaws players like Matt Kavanagh and Noah Molnar.

He was determined to try out again in 2018.

Having been turned away several times already, why was it so important that he continue to push for a spot on the Outlaws roster?

"Playing lacrosse is my life. In my opinion, it's the same," he said. "You have some obstacle or something you have to figure out. There is any hope or you desire something, just do it. So last year, I made the season roster. I made my debut as a Japanese lacrosse player. I'm so honored, but at that time, I was thinking I'm not only the first Asian or Japanese professional lacrosse player who played a game, I was an Outlaw. I was not a guest. I was a part of them. I was on the team with them. I was so honored, but I just want to win as an Outlaw."

Iwamoto made the roster in 2018, and he was selected to the practice roster for 2019 (he did not have to attend the open tryout in 2019).

His work ethic and determination were not lost on Cohen.

"For open tryouts, he was in Japan. We had a tryout in California. He flew out to California," he said. "He flew back to Japan, and I didn't know he wasn't living in the States. I told him, 'We'd like to see you again in Denver.' He flew back out to Denver four days later. It's a guy you can't deny how much he wants it. He's living his summers in Denver, seeing shots. The best part about Kai has been seeing him integrate himself into the Denver lacrosse community. A bunch of people know him. Kids know him. He's coaching goalies. He's doing all this different stuff in Denver, which has been fantastic to see him integrate himself into the community."

With Jack Kelly, the starting goalie, and Dillon Ward, the backup goalie, playing for the United States and Canada, respectively, in the 2018 FIL World Championships, the Outlaws needed a goalie for their July 22 game against the Rattlers.

Iwamoto was promoted to the active roster and started his first game. He played 49 minutes and 6 seconds, allowing ten goals (including one two-pointer) and making 11 saves. While he wasn't the goalie of record, the Outlaws did lose the game. Iwamoto was disappointed, but he was honored to have earned the chance to play, let alone make history.

Denver eventually won the championship that season, and with Kelly injured, Iwamoto was dressed as the backup for the victory.

Not surprisingly, Iwamoto has earned the respect of his teammates.

"He's awesome," Ward said. "You see Kai week-in and week-out at practice and what he means to the team and the raw passion he has for the sport. It's incredible. He'll be on the field until he's kicked off. He cares about the guys on our team. He just wants to get better. It's awesome to see him. He's a fantastic goalie. It's a cool story. It's great to share it with him. He plays a huge role in getting our guys ready before games. You have to beg him to get out of the net."

His journey to Major League Lacrosse was a long one, both literally and metaphorically. He couldn't be happier, however, to be a part of it.

"The biggest surprise here is I'm still not perfect at English, but all American lacrosse players are super nice to me, I think, because I love the sport they love," he said. "We have something in common, and we can be friends. I can do this everywhere on Earth, even Europe, or Korea, or wherever. To play lacrosse internationally is different. I want more players to go abroad. From the United States, you're the best, but you can make a different experience in Europe or Asia. They all love lacrosse, and they all love people who play lacrosse. People in Denver, they're super nice to me. I love all parts of lacrosse right now. I probably will keep playing as long as possible."

While the Outlaws game against the Cannons five days before the Mile High Fourth of July game was in Boston, it felt like a home game for one of Denver's players: Max Adler.

While the Cannons usually have a good showing of fans rooting for the home team, when Adler came to town, there was a whole cheering section wearing shirts with "Adler" across the back and rooting for the third-year face-off specialist. They even were on the field behind him when he did a postgame interview with Lax Sports Network.

"I mean these are guys that came to all my Bentley lacrosse games, like really supported me there," he said prior to the Fourth of July game. "My dad did a lot with the shirts and everything like that. After the game, they were telling me, 'I've been to Boston Celtics games, Bruins games, Patriots games,' but they said that was, by far, the most fun they'd ever had. A lot of them were friends of friends to like maybe their girlfriends who don't super watch or are fans of lacrosse. This was the first lacrosse game they'd ever seen, and they had the most fun ever. It was great to see how much they enjoyed it, and obviously, it was so special to me to have everyone there, to have my coach [Bentley head coach Jim Murphy] get inducted into the [Eastern Massachusetts] Hall of Fame right before the game, that just made it extra, extra special, and it was unbelievable."

Adler grew up in Florida and played a little lacrosse in rec leagues during his middle school years, but it didn't become a serious sport for him until his freshman year at Northfield Mount Herman (Massachusetts). Not only did he pick up the sport late, he also didn't play during his junior year, which is typically an important year to get recruited.

Adler's top sport was wrestling, and while there was some interest at the collegiate level, injuries kept him from going down that path. He opted to go to Bentley University in Waltham, Massachusetts and majored in corporate financing and accounting. He talked to Murphy about joining the team (which plays in NCAA Division 2), and he allowed Adler to tryout.

As a freshman, Adler was the fifth face-off specialist out of five. He played in seven games, winning five of seven face-offs. He quickly ascended the depth chart, however, and was a starter his sophomore season; he never looked back. Adler won 69.2 percent of his face-offs during his tenure at Bentley, was a three-time All-New England selection, two-time All-Conference selection, and was a Second Team All-America selection.

Despite his success at Bentley, there wsn't a large number of Division 2 and Division 3 players at the professional level. Adler was drafted in the seventh round of the 2017 MLL Collegiate Draft by the Denver Outlaws.

"Adler, I knew and watched," Seaman said, "and saw him grow and said, 'Man, this kid could do it.'"

He played in three games as a rookie, scoring one goal and winning 55.4 percent of his face-offs. He was slated to be the backup to MLL All-Star Thomas Kelly again in 2018, but Kelly missed the May 19 game due to an injury. Adler stepped in and won 24 of 34 face-offs, impressing the Denver staff. The Outlaws traded Kelly to the New York Lizards for a first-round draft pick and made Adler the starter.

In seven games in 2018, Adler ranked third in the league with a 57.9 face-off winning percentage. He helped the Outlaws win the 2018 MLL Championship.

In the championship contest, he won 15 of 29 face-offs despite suffering a knee injury early in the game. Nothing – no injury, no opponent – was going to slow Adler down at that point.

"I remember me and Mikie [Schlosser] last year before the championship were talking," he said. "We were both like, 'This is so important to us. Every time I step on the field, I'm perfectly ok with dying if it means winning the game.'"

Adler opted to stay with the Outlaws for the 2019 season. Not only was he the top face-off guy for the defending champions, he became one of the faces of the entire league.

In addition to his career in MLL, Adler works for ESPN as a financial analyst. For the Outlaws, Adler is a competitive player, but he also plays to honor those that have helped him along the way.

"I mean, to think that I would be a starter, to think that we would win a championship and that I would be a part of the team and everything like that and actually playing, it's not like I dreamed of that when I was younger. I never thought that was a possibility in any way, so I try not to get like too caught up," he said. "I play for those people who really believed in me along the way. There's definitely some lonely mornings in the offseason and after work where it's like, I just worked a full day and it's tough, but those are the people that really motivate me, most importantly, my teammates, just because that's who I play for. We all want to win. We're all going to that same goal."

Over the years, when players have been asked what their favorite visiting stadium or city to play in was, many responded by saying, "Denver." The fan support the team received and getting to play at Broncos Stadium at Mile High were appealing features for players.

Thanks to a partnership with Altitude Sports and Entertainment, a television network that services the Rocky Mountain region, the Outlaws were one of the more recognizable MLL franchises.

"I got [a text] after the Boston game," said Cohen, "that said, 'Hey, I'm sitting in Arizona and the Outlaws are on the T.V. at the bar.'"

It helped that Pat Bowlen – who owned the NFL's Denver Broncos prior to his death on June 13, 2019 – was the principal owner of the Outlaws, and the team shared resources with the Broncos.

For those that are lucky enough to play for the Outlaws, it's an organization they never want to leave. The coaching staff is a prime example of this.

Seaman joined the Outlaws in 2012 as the team's general manager. Cohen, the current general manager, was in his 13th season with the organization, and assistant coaches John Grant Jr. and Matt Bocklet were both former Outlaws players.

Grant Jr. played in the inaugural Major League Lacrosse season and joined the Outlaws via trade in 2014. He played for the team for three seasons, helping Denver win its first MLL championship, before being traded during the 2016 season. He retired after that year and rejoined the Outlaws as the team's offensive coordinator. Days before the start of the 2019 season, Grant Jr. came out of retirement to be a player-coach for Denver; this not only helped the Outlaws on the field (he scored the first goal of the 2019 MLL season), it also was a treat for the younger players to be teammates with an individual they idolized while growing up.

"He's such a good brain out there and does such a good job redistributing the ball and facilitating everybody and occasionally gets in there and makes some sweet plays as well. It's fun to be a part of," Schlosser said. "I was a huge fan of him growing up. It's cool. It was cool to meet him. It was cool to be coached by him, and now, it's even cooler to play with him and be a teammate with him."

Bocklet played for the Washington Bayhawks in his rookie season of 2008 before joining the Denver Outlaws for training camp in 2009. Eleven seasons later, Bocklet retired after 144 games (a franchise record), three championships, and five All-Star Game appearances. He was brought back to be the team's defensive coordinator for the 2019 season.

"After being a part of [the Outlaws] for so long, I didn't want to give that up," Bocklet said. "It's given me so much and moved me out here to Denver, and it's a special organization. It starts from the top with Pat Bowlen and everything he believed in with the Broncos. Then, when he started the Outlaws, he made sure we were running the same exact way and trying to be number one in everything we do. With attendance, our fans, and now winning three championships, I think we've really done our part to follow up on what Pat Bowlen wanted from this organization."

Denver had been a place of family for Bocklet. He had enjoyed the time he spent in what he calls an "ego-less" locker room, creating great relationships with his teammates, and he also got to play with his blood relatives. Bocklet has teamed with his younger brother, Chris; his older brother, Mike; and his younger cousin, Graham.

Through the years, Bocklet has been around for a lot of Major League Lacrosse's missteps and challenging times. Between his first and second year, the league went from 10 teams to six. He saw the league rise back to nine teams, only to fall back to six after he retired.

Despite the problems around the league, Denver continued to carry on strongly. The three championships were tied for second-most in league history and were tied with the Chesapeake Bayhawks for the most since 2006, the team's debut season. Additionally, from 2013 through 2018, the Outlaws led the league in average attendance. Yes, those numbers were benefitted by the Fourth of July game, greatly skewing the average, but other teams held firework games and the results were not similar in any way.

Bocklet credited the team's front office for making sure that playing for the Outlaws always felt like playing for a professional team.

"There's something special about this place. To have our own locker room at Mile High Stadium, an NFL stadium, no team has that," he said. "The front office and ownership, when they're taking care of the players, you feel that. There's a little extra sense of pride in wanting to do well because you know they're doing everything they can for you as a player. When you have that backup, you're always going to put a great product on the field, and that's helped us come together as a team."

The attendance for the 2019 Mile High Fourth of July game was 26,210 people. Those at the game were very dedicated fans who sat through three weather delays due to lightning in the area. Despite the poor weather and the long time between the start of the game and its finish, the fans stayed, and they were treated to an Outlaws come-from-behind win, 14-13, and a fireworks show.

Among all the fans, one superfan stood out: JoJo War Drummer. He stood on the sidelines in a custom Outlaws jersey, a black top hat, team-colored face paint ("war paint" as he called it), his drum, and a conch shell.

As the game was played on the field, he banged on his drum in order to motivate the Outlaws players and get in the heads of the opposition. The players from all teams know him, and they are fans.

"JoJo is awesome," Cannons goalie Nick Marrocco said. "He definitely brings the intensity, which is awesome to see."

"Superfans in any sport, especially if they are prevalent enough that they have a reputation where they become their own entity, is unbelievable. It is so important for the team's culture and fan zone to have their own leaders," Cannons defender James Fahey said. "JoJo definitely has an independent identity."

"He's the most passionate lacrosse fan I have ever met," Bocklet said. "It only helps bring positive vibes and energy to the sport, and that's all he wants. He just wants to see Colorado teams do well and kids be successful in lacrosse, which is why he's a great fan."

"He's the man," Adler said. "He's at every single one of our games, just like really adds a lot of energy to our team. You can really hear the drum going. It's awesome."

Joseph Mares was first introduced to the sport of lacrosse as a child living in Los Angeles. He and his brother went to the Olympics held in the city in 1984 and saw guys playing the game in the parking lot. They told the boys about the game's origins, and he said he felt an instant connection because he, too, was of Native American descent. He said he went back to his Pop Warner football coaches, asking where he could play the game, but they either didn't know about it or said the only places they knew of that played lacrosse were at private schools in Malibu or Beverly Hills.

He forgot about lacrosse until he moved to Denver in the early 90s.

"I was like yes, yes, yes, it's here! It's here," he said.

JoJo had been drumming since he was a little child; his parents took him to pow wows to learn about his culture. He said in 2005, he took his drum to a youth tournament in Denver.

"I started hitting the drum, and then right away, the kids started picking up their step. They started pepping up," he said. "The coaches, the referees, and the parents started liking it. I stopped playing, and I noticed they were stagnant. I was like, 'Wait a minute.' I started hitting the drum, and they started picking up their pace, both teams, offense and defense. Coaches started getting into it. I was like, 'Whoa!' I did it again, and I was like, 'Ok, this is no coincidence.'"

JoJo was excited to see the professional game come to Denver in 2006. He attended games as a regular fan early on. In the team's second season, he saw someone on the sidelines that looked "official," and he flagged him down to ask about drumming at the games. That individual turned out to be Mac Freeman, the team's president, and he asked JoJo to bring his drum to the next game. He started drumming in the stands, and the next season, the team asked him to move to the sidelines.

In addition to drumming at Outlaws games, JoJo plays for the men's and women's teams at the University of Denver and for youth tournaments in the area; before the Outlaws game against the Bayhawks, he had spent the day drumming at the World Series of Youth Lacrosse, which was held nearby at Dick's Sporting Goods Park. He appreciats the work the Outlaws do in the community, and he is a fan of his hometown teams.

"I see they recognize true lacrosse fans want their home team to win," he said. "That's what sports is. It's fun. For example, if you go to the Harlem Globetrotters, I really like it. It's a lot of fun, good entertainment, but then, when it comes to the Denver Nuggets or something like that, you want to root for your home team more, not just for entertainment. It's something extra. That's what brings out the extra passion when you have the home field."

Even his young son, a lacrosse player and fan, recognized how important the Outlaws were to JoJo.

"My son, GT, his name is Glen Tewaaraton. He just turned 8," he said. "I said, 'Man, I hope you go to the Denver Outlaws.' He said, 'Dad, what if I go to another team?' I was like, 'Oh, man. Dangit.' I said, 'I might have to drum for your team. I don't know.' Then he goes, 'Dad, the Denver Outlaws are your team. You're still my dad. You drum for your team.' I said, 'Thank you. We can hug before and after the game.' That hit me right there. I thought he was putting me on the spot, but he knows how passionate I am for the Denver Outlaws."

JoJo became a staple of Outlaws games. For some, he's even more recognizable than the players. During the weather delay before the start of the game, JoJo played his drum for the Team Israel group of players that played in the World Series of Lacrosse earlier in the day, and he had them dancing. During the postgame fireworks, a young female fan came up to him and excitedly asked to take a selfie with him. He even had his own trading card as a part of the MLL set that Parkside Collectibles issued for the 2019 season.

Outside of the time he spends at Outlaws games, JoJo had a lot going on in his life. He is a husband, a father, a youth lacrosse coach, and a youth lacrosse referee. He also had his own podcast, "A Cup of JoJo … War Drummer Ways!" Despite his other responsibilities, he remained a dedicated fan and attendee of Outlaws games. For some fans, the games are a few hours of entertainment. For JoJo, Outlaws games mean so much more.

"I have four kids. I have my oldest and youngest are boys. My two in the middle are girls," he said. "My two boys, one lives here in the Denver area, which we talk often. My little one, GT, he lives at home with my wife and I. My two girls have been missing for a long time. Drumming for lacrosse and the appreciation I get from the Denver Outlaws players and fans and everything like that from the Denver Outlaws games and everything else I do, it helps give me medicine to keep going.

"Literally, every day a piece of my heart breaks because I don't know where my girls are," he added. "I know they're somewhere here.

I don't know where. They're not in Colorado. I don't know where my ex-girlfriend took them. She's hiding them from me. It's hard. Many times in the nighttime, I find it hard to even sleep. Every week I go about [two nights] where I don't sleep that night because I wonder where they are."

While talking about his children, JoJo recalled a time roughly sixteen years ago where he and a friend were jumped outside of a billiards bar. While he didn't realize it at the time, he said the doctors informed him he was stabbed 14 times. Both he and his friend survived, but he still had scars from the attack.

While it was a scary scenario, one that hurt physically, he said it pales in comparison to how hurt he is without his daughters in his life.

"The pain I feel for my daughters missing well surpasses that," he said. "The medicine of lacrosse helps me overcome that."

He said he hoped for reunification one day. In the meantime, he builds his relationships with his two sons, and he is flattered by the support of the Outlaws organization and the players in Major League Lacrosse.

"The Bayhawks, the Cannons, all the other teams, how they appreciate what I do for my Denver Outlaws, that really means so much," he said. "It keeps me going."

4.
JULY 7
BOSTON AT DALLAS

Christian Carson-Banister: Jerome Miron/Pretty Instant

*"**What** brings you to Dallas?" the concierge at the downtown hotel asked.*
"I'm here for the professional lacrosse game Sunday, the Dallas Rattlers MLL game," I responded.
"Oh," replied the concierge. "I didn't even know we had a team."

The night before the game against the Cannons, the Dallas Rattlers held practice at Prestonwood Christian Academy in Plano, Texas. It is a high school, but high school football stadiums in Texas are much larger than elsewhere in the country.

As the players prep for practice, one man is wearing sweatpants, holding sticks, and answering questions from surrounding players and personnel.

"Hi, I'm Bill. I work with the team," he said.

"He doesn't just work with the team," interjected Austin Lee, the Rattlers Brand Manager. "He's Bill Goren. He's the president of the team."

Goren was named team president when the Rattlers moved from Rochester to Dallas in December 2017. A Texas native, Goren had no prior experience with lacrosse. What he did have, however, was an extensive background in professional sports. His career began in the sales department with Major League Baseball's Los Angeles Dodgers for five years before he took a position as the senior director of ticket sales with the Houston Astros for seven years, which included the team's run to the World Series in 2005. He also held leadership positions with the Austin Toros (the San Antonio Spurs G-League affiliate) and the Frisco Rough Riders (the Double-A affiliate of the Texas Rangers).

He arrived at his position with the Rattlers with several ideas, but one of the most important concepts was to treat players and employees like they worked for a professional organization; it seems like an obvious thought, since the Rattlers do play in Major League Lacrosse, but the execution did not always match the concept.

The Chicago Machine relocated to Rochester and assumed the Rattlers logo, colors, and history in 2011. While the players enjoyed success on the field, the team struggled to maintain a home stadium, playing in three different stadiums in the final three years; there were consistent concerns of where the team could find practice space or if they'd have the proper equipment to have practice; and from 2013 through 2017, the season always ended with a rumor the team would be relocated once again.

"In Rochester, I got the impression they weren't always treated that way," he said. "The reason they were such a good, close team is they had this chip on their shoulder. They were the have-nots of the league. They came here, and we gave them a first-class facility. We do a lot of little things to make them feel special. We make sure every game we provide them with some other swag that's Rattlers related, so they continue to wear and share the brand. Like today, we pick up all our players at the airport ourselves. I made five runs to the airport today by myself just picking up players. It's a way to build that bond. I'm not trying to be cheap and not spend money on Uber. At the end of the day, they know I care enough to drive there and [Rattlers Brand Director] Austin [Lee] cares enough, and [Rattlers Director of Operations] Laura [Bolton] cares enough, that we are very hands on when it comes to treating these guys how they should be treated.

"These guys are flying from all over the United States Friday," he added. "They're going to run through a practice Saturday night, run through a practice Sunday morning, and go. It was important for me to treat them, because they're sacrificing so much, in my opinion, to treat them like major league players. When you treat them that way, they carry themselves that way."

That philosophy extends not only to the players but to the staff as well.

"When we started putting it together, I was like, 'Look, I want to make my staff feel like they're part of this,'" he said. "I've been on that side where we never felt like we were part of it. We're expendable. The players are the ones that are important. This way, I'm going to make my staff feel important. We took them to championship when we went last year. We gave them jerseys. We try to embrace our staff."

One of the first decisions Goren had to make about his staff was who would be the head coach. Tim Soudan, a former NLL and MLL player (he played three seasons with the Rochester Rattlers beginning in the inaugural season in 2001), coached the team from 2011 to 2017 but was not moving to Dallas with the team.

Goren was tasked with hiring the new coach, but without any lacrosse background, he struggled to find a person he felt would be the right fit. That is, until he talked to Bill Warder on the phone.

"I talked to Warder for about 10 minutes with his background in Major League Lacrosse and the Rochester Rattlers, blue collar," Goren said. "I'm wearing sweatpants. I work with the team. I do anything that needs to be done. Warder is the exact same way.

"I talked to him two or three times about 20 minutes each time and was like, 'I love this guy,'" he added. "He's the guy that can build this team."

Warder previously played four years in the NLL as well as in MLL's inaugural season. He had two stints as an assistant coach with the Rochester Rattlers, from 2006 to 2008 and then from 2011 to 2017.

He was thrilled with an opportunity to be a head coach in the league.

"You're given so few opportunities in life to pursue and do what you love, whether that's lacrosse or whatever it might be," he said. "I started at a really young age. I caught the bug at four or five-years-old. Hey, I love this game. It was something that's in your DNA. Whether it's kindergarten or the pro level or high school or JV, being lucky enough to be involved with the sport in some way is really connective. It's just a passion for this sport."

In Warder's first season, the team finished first in the regular season standings with an 11-3 record and reached the championship game for the third time in five seasons. The team was once again unable to get over the hump, however, losing to the Outlaws, 16-12.

Goren would need Warder's ability to build a team in 2019, however. With the arrival of the PLL, many of Dallas's core players – including both starting goalie John Galloway and backup goalie Blaze Riorden, leading scorer Jordan Wolf, two of the next three top scorers in Ty Thompson and Ned Crotty, and starting defenders and former Defensive Players of the Year Mike Manley and Joel White – moved to the new league. Dallas went into the 2019 season with many holes to fill in the lineup.

Things didn't get off to a good start. Prior to the July 7 game against Boston, Dallas lost each of its first five games, several in frustrating fashion. In the season opener, the Rattlers blew a halftime lead against the Chesapeake Bayhawks. The following week, they spotted the Cannons nine goals before scoring their first.

Warder was confident his team would eventually right the ship. They just needed more time together.

"We say it's a game of runs," he said. "Teams go on winning streaks. Teams go on a losing streak. Teams score five goals in a row. It's similar. Every year, you hit the reset button.

"The players change a lot here and there over a 20-year period, but still, the players that come, whether they come out of college right into it, they compete to play," he added. "Whether it's year one or year 20, these players come every game with a ton of energy. That's been constant every year."

Warder has been involved in the game of lacrosse for many years. His grandfather was a captain for Hobart and gave him his first stick at the age of five. He was a ball boy for Hobart in the early stages of the program's streak of 12 consecutive NCAA Division 3 championships.

Throughout the wins, the losses, and the travel mishaps, what he loves about the sport is the people in it.

"People who play the game are really passionate about it and want to help and serve and be friends with other people who have lacrosse sticks in their hands," he said. "Whether that's in Dallas or Boston or Denver or Atlanta, if you have a lacrosse stick in your hand and your car breaks down on the side of the road, someone is probably going to stop."

On Goren's bio on the Rattlers web site, it said, "With a clear focus on the community, Goren will drive outreach throughout North Dallas, work to expand the game of lacrosse across Texas and provide the highest level of service and entertainment to fans."

One way the Rattlers are working with the community is with a youth advisory board. The organization communicates with the board – made up of representatives from the local youth lacrosse programs (Goren said there were about 15 programs participating) – for feedback about what is working, what isn't, and how to form a tighter bond with the community.

Another way the Rattlers go about expanding outreach in the community is actually having players from the area and physically available for promotion.

The Rattlers have several players on the roster either from Texas or working in Texas, including MLL veteran Zack Greer. Initially selected by the Long Island Lizards with the third overall pick in 2009 MLL Collegiate Draft, his time in Major League Lacrosse was sporadic. He was with Long Island in 2009 and 2010, sat out a few seasons, and then joined the Denver Outlaws in 2013 and 2014. While he scored a career-high 28 points in 11 games in 2013, he played in only four games in Denver's 2014 championship season. Then Greer disappeared from the league.

He was not on the league's radar until he met Goren at the Dallas Rattlers initial press conference.

"I'm at The Star. We've got our conference room ready. We've got the table there, and I didn't like how the shirts were folded. I just went and picked them up and started rolling them," he said. "This guy comes up and is like, 'What are you guys doing?' I go, 'We're going to announce a Major League Lacrosse team. Have you ever heard of Major League Lacrosse?' He was like, 'Yeah.'

"Then, I see that same guy talking to our commissioner," he added. "The commissioner comes up and says, 'Hey, Bill, come meet this guy,' and I was like, 'Yeah, I just met him over there.' He's like, 'This is Zack Greer,' and I was like, ok. Without a big lacrosse background, I was like, 'Hey, Zack.' They said he played in the league. So, I called Warder, our coach, and said, 'Hey, I met a guy named Zack who played in the league.' He said, 'Is he in shape?'"

Greer had gone from California to Texas and was working at The Star, where Goren and Greer connected. With interest from both sides, the Rattlers planned to take Greer in the annual supplemental draft. Since he hadn't played since 2014, Dallas was able to select Greer in the fifth round.

"When we got him, we got a couple calls [from other teams] saying he's not going to play," Goren said. "They thought we were idiots. They realize now he lives here, and he's a great player for us."

He played in only four games in the 2018 season, but he became a more regular player in the 2019 season.

While Greer lived and worked in Texas, he is originally from Canada. In addition to having Greer local, the Rattlers had a few players who are from the Dallas/Fort Worth area, including attackman Bryce Wasserman and goalie Christian Carson-Banister.

Bryce Wasserman is from Southlake, Texas and went to high school at Grapevine Faith Christian School, which is less than 30 miles away from the Ford Center at The Star. Christian Carson-Banister attended Jesuit College Preparatory School of Dallas, 15 miles away from The Star.

Of course, neither the Ford Center at The Star nor the Dallas Rattlers existed when Wasserman and Carson-Banister were growing up. Lacrosse wasn't very popular in Texas, either. Both found their way to the Creator's Game, however.

"It was sixth grade and the baseball practice fields in South Lake at the sports complex, the outfield backs up to where the lacrosse fields were," Wasserman said. "So, literally, I was sitting in right field, bored out of my mind, and just looked over the fence and saw the lacrosse practice going on, and it looked like the most fun thing.

"My dad played football at Towson, so he had known a couple guys that played lacrosse," he added. "He reached out to them saying, 'Hey, my son wants to play,' and they sent a whole care package, and that was that. I switched over the next week and never picked up a baseball glove again."

Unlike Wasserman, Carson-Banister's father did play lacrosse, and that's how he got into the sport.

"My dad played college tennis, and he was transferring to [the University of North Texas]," he said. "It was a coincidence, but the tennis program got cut the year he enrolled. He wanted to pick up something, so they had a club lacrosse program, and that's how he got into the sport, and consequently, it's how I got in, because of him."

As Carson-Banister and Wasserman both navigated the Texas lacrosse scene, they wound up taking similar paths. After successful high school careers (Carson-Banister was All-District as a junior, and Wasserman was an All-American and three-time team Offensive MVP), both players played collegiate lacrosse for new programs: Carson-Banister at Boston University and Wasserman at Monmouth University.

BU and Monmouth both became Division 1 programs in 2014, with Carson-Banister joining the Terriers for their inaugural season while Wasserman joined the Hawks for their second year.

Carson-Banister said the new programs provided opportunity, especially for players who come from outside the typical hotbeds.

"I just think it's great opportunities to shine early," he said. "That's one of the things with these new programs. They bring in a new class. You get an opportunity to be on a roster with 40 other guys that are predominately freshmen. I think it's having an opportunity to play early. It's really difficult when a lot of these bigger programs, you go there, you get buried, and you have to grind your way through for about two, three years to see the field. In a new program, it's day one. There's a difference there."

At Boston University, Carson-Banister earned the starting goalie position immediately, even winning the team's MVP award in his freshman season.

He earned national recognition in his senior season, being named to the USILA and Inside Lacrosse All-American teams as well as winning the Patriot League Goaltender of the Year award. He set program records for save percentage in a season and goals against average in a season; in fact, through 2020, Carson-Banister still owned the top four spots in save percentage for a season and goals against average in a season.

Carson-Banister did not land with an MLL team after his senior year, but Dallas added him in the 2018 supplemental draft. In his first season with the Rattlers, Carson-Banister served as the third goalie behind backup Blaze Riorden and starter John Galloway, the player he watched on YouTube while growing up and attempted to model his style after.

"Both of them were incredible goalies," Carson-Banister said. "They're two of the best goalies I've had the pleasure to play with. To see their approach, two different styles, I learned a little bit from both of them. They each had great advice that has helped me tremendously. Being able to see them play live, Blaze and I are closer in years but more so Galloway and being able to be on the same field, it was a cool moment."

Carson-Banister can see what many would view as negatives: the travel, the small salary, being a backup, losing games. He doesn't let those things get in the way of or supersede his love of the game.

"When you love something, everything about it is enjoyable," he said. "Playing this game is not about showing off to other people and trying to impress others, so that's why it never bothered me. For me, it was such a personal experience. It was such an escape. Lacrosse has always been an escape for me. I get self-fulfillment from seeing the ball and trying to stop it, and, again, it's such a relaxing and almost really calming experience."

The beginning of Wasserman's MLL career also began in 2018, and it started in similar fashion: he wasn't playing.

Wasserman was drafted by the Denver Outlaws with the number 62 pick in the 2018 MLL Draft, the first player from Monmouth University drafted into the league. It was the latest in a long line of firsts for Wasserman at Monmouth.

At the Jersey Shore school, Wasserman was part of the program's first MAAC regular season and tournament championship teams. He also graduated first in school history in career goals (99), game-winning goals (9), hat tricks (14), assists (50), and points (149), as well as goals in a season (34), assists in a season (17), points in a season (51), goals in a game (6), assists in a game (5), and points in a game (7).

"That was kind of our mentality when we went into it," he said. "We wanted to be the footsteps for other Monmouth teams to follow. Other programs, say a Duke or wherever, we all want to follow in the footsteps of this team. At Monmouth, we wanted to be the team other people followed in the footsteps of."

Despite Wasserman's scoring domination at Monmouth, he landed on a veteran-heavy team in Denver that was difficult to break into, especially at the attack position; Eric Law, Matt Kavanagh, and rookie Chris Cloutier all played in the 2018 MLL All-Star Game, while Kylor Bellistri and Wes Berg were also high-scoring options.

With zero games to his credit, Wasserman made a difficult decision: he asked the Outlaws for his release.

"I told him, 'Coach Seaman, I know I can do this. I want to go try. I understand you don't need me. Please, just let me try to go find my home,'" he said. "It was that mentality that I knew I just needed one shot."

As one of the last two players selected in the Collegiate Draft and no game tape to go off of, there was no guarantee Wasserman would find that home. He reached out to every team, fearing no one would reciprocate.

Ohio and head coach Bear Davis were willing to give him an opportunity, however. The Machine – the defending league champion – were undergoing a season of turmoil. League MVP Tom Schreiber was injured; none of the team's top players – Schreiber, Marcus Holman, Peter Baum, and Kyle Harrison – played a full 14-game season for various reasons.

Wasserman played in Ohio's final three games of the year. In three games, he scored eight goals and added two assists. It was a small sample size, but it was enough to show what Wasserman was capable of at the professional level. Before folding, Davis was ready to make Wasserman a focal point of the Machine and build the team around him.

"He's smart and embracing an opportunity right now," Davis said prior to the start of the 2019 season. "He did that from day one. His first or second rep, he scored and never looked back. He's a confident young man. You have to be to go from a guy drafted pretty close to last in the draft and wasn't getting an opportunity to get in the game and make the most of it. He grabbed the bull by the horns."

When the Ohio Machine franchise ceased operations prior to the 2019 season, Wasserman was once again without a professional home, but it was his geographic home team that called with another opportunity.

Not only was Wasserman thankful to be on another team, he was excited to bring all his knowledge and talent back home.

"It couldn't be more special to me to wear Dallas across my chest for one, and for two, a 12-year-old kid who just picked up a lacrosse stick, they can drive 20 minutes down the road, look at me on the field, and point and say, 'I want to be that. That's what I want to be,'" he said. "It is special to me to represent Dallas and be the person kids look up to."

Despite being the newest market in Major League Lacrosse, and despite Dallas not being a traditional lacrosse hotbed, Warder said the enthusiasm of the fans in the first season was very impressive.

Dallas's July 7 game against the Boston Cannons, however, had a less than ideal start time of 12:30 on a Sunday afternoon. Not only did that interfere with church times for many in the Dallas-Fort Worth area, it was also immediately following the 2019 FIFA Women's World Cup final, which the United States National Team played in.

The reported attendance for the game was 2,773, a light crowd to say the least. Die-hard fans made sure not to miss the game, though, and as they walked through the door, they were greeted by the team's cheerleaders and new mascot, Fang.

Included in the crowd was the Kovacs Family: Kenneth, Nicolle, their son Kody, and Kody's friend, Colin.

The family was introduced to lacrosse while in the hospital with Kody following a surgery he underwent. They were flipping through the channels and came across a documentary about lacrosse.

"After watching it and watching when they were discussing how the Canadians and Indians and everyone on the east coast, when they start to go into the history and explaining the sport and how serious they took it, and how they settled conflict and wars with a lacrosse game," said Nicolle, "and the more we watched it, we saw so much soccer in it, but we saw the physical contact and the ball movement and how fast paced it was. We fell in love with it."

Kody started playing lacrosse in fourth grade. When the 2017 MLL Championship Game was played in Dallas, the Kovacs Family made sure to be in attendance. Even though Kody was injured and in a boot, the game was memorable for many reasons.

"The environment. It's family," he said when asked about his favorite part. He also scored some great memorabilia. "Whenever the Ohio Machine guy broke his stick, I got the broken end of the shaft."

When the news broke that the Rattlers were moving from Rochester to Dallas, Kenneth and Nicolle bought Kody season tickets as a Christmas gift.

It has been an experience they don't regret.

"The players come up and are a part of the event," Kenneth said. "They come up to the stands and see all the kids and the parents or whoever wants to see them. They take extra time to sign autographs and have a small discussion with you, which makes it even better.

"These players, they're not paid like the NFL players, but they still take their time after the game, which they could walk off and go home because they have other jobs to support their living," he added. "That's a big deal when you know that's going on."

"There's a respect and love for the game and everyone else," Nicolle said. "We don't see any fighting. The whole environment is more professional here. You don't see people arguing with each other or people having a bad attitude. It's very positive. I've heard other parents standing in line at halftime to get a cold beer. Everyone says how nice it is. It's a positive environment."

That positivity extends beyond just the families, as well. A group of young professionals came together to form the Rat Pack in support of the Rattlers.

Matt Hawkins is one of the five members of the fan group, and he described how excited he and his friends were to have professional lacrosse in Dallas.

"We all played high school lacrosse here in Dallas. We all played at Allen, just down the road. A lot of us went to college and played lacrosse in college, mostly Big 12 schools," he said. "Moving back home, we all got jobs in Dallas. To know the Rochester team came here to Dallas, we were stoked. We said we were going to get season tickets. We want to be big fans. We want to be front row and bring the hype and bring the energy. We think it's really great there's a team here, especially in a community like Frisco that's growing so fast, not just the businesses moving here, but lacrosse in North Texas has taken off. It's big in the northeast, but when we played, we didn't know what the hell we were doing. We had to drive out to Louisiana. We had to pay for all of our stuff. As young professionals in the DFW area, we were stoked to have a local team to support."

Against the Cannons, Hawkins, Tim Massey, Ben Walker, and Lane Broadway sat in the front row behind the Rattlers bench. Typically, Andrew Goldston joins them, but he couldn't make the early Sunday game, so the group brought another friend to take his place.

Among their chants throughout the game, the guys created their own chant whenever Dallas scores. After a goal, they bang on the wall in front of them, then pick their hands up and hiss like a snake (think in the rhythm of Queen's "We Will Rock You").

Although they were recently out of college and enjoy adult beverages before and during the game, they also want to make sure they aren't ruining the experience for anyone around them.

"We get the kids involved doing our chants and cheers, doing very PG chants, but once we get the kids involved in the game, that's what makes it fun for us," Hawkins said. "We want to get everybody pumped about lacrosse. We want people coming back and cheering along with us. Getting the crowd involved as much as we can is my favorite thing."

While they hope to get the fans involved and supporting the home team, that doesn't mean they are afraid to heckle the opposition.

"My buddy, Tim, he was heckling [Paul] Rabil all game last year to the point where he made his own league to get away from us," Walker said in jest. "I think that was pretty good. It was dead silent in the stadium, one of those times the music cut out between goals, and Tim, out of nowhere, yelled 'Rabil, we love you.' He looked right at us, and Tim goes, 'Not!' Everyone was laughing. That was his last game in Frisco. We started a Rabil chant every time he touched the ball. He had like one goal in a playoff game. That was one of the best [moments]."

The fellow fans weren't the only ones that appreciated the enthusiasm the Rat Pack brings with them. Dallas's front office, including Goren, enjoyed the passion this group of fans brought to every home game. Goren even stopped by during halftime to say hello.

"Since day one, it's been a lot of fun," Massey said. "The first time we bought season tickets, we met everyone from merchandising to sales to the president of the team."

"As far as Bill and those guys recognizing us, the big wigs of the Rattlers, it's pretty cool," Walker added. "Our goal is to get additional super fans, maybe honorary members of the Rat Pack, and fill the section out with a whole bunch of people enjoying the sport and heckling."

There are a number of lacrosse fans in Dallas, but football is king in Texas, and the Dallas Cowboys are one of the most storied franchises in the National Football League thanks to their five Super Bowls. *Forbes* ranks the most valuable sports teams every year, and the Dallas Cowboys ranked first every year since 2016.

Cowboys fans have had the pleasure of rooting for a myriad of Hall of Famers, including icons like Troy Aikman, Emmitt Smith, Michael Irvin, Deion Sanders, and Charles Haley.

One Hall of Famer they did not get to root for on the Cowboys was linebacker Junior Seau. Most known for his time with the San Diego Chargers, Seau also played with the Miami Dolphins and New England Patriots. He was a 12-time Pro Bowl selection, the 1992 NFL Defensive Player of the Year, and won the Man of the Year award in 1992.

He did not get to enjoy being enshrined in the Hall of Fame, however, passing away in 2012 at 43-years-old. He also did not get to see his son, Jake, follow in his footsteps as a professional athlete as a midfielder for the Rattlers.

"I think he'd be proud," Seau said of his dad. "I think he'd be excited I could keep playing. That's the biggest thing for any guy that moves into the league and moves up. It's just another opportunity to play the sport you love, so I think that would be exciting for him."

Seau started playing lacrosse in seventh grade. His social studies teacher coached club and high school lacrosse in San Diego, and he brought the football and basketball player to practice to introduce him to the sport.

He was not a natural, but that's what he liked about the sport.

"It was something completely new, something I never really had seen or heard of," he said. "I was also super bad at it, so it was something for my competitive side. I started playing a little later, and I was playing with a bunch of guys that had been playing a couple years. When I was younger, I was definitely motivated just to get better and grow the skills."

Seau played college lacrosse at Duke University. As a freshman in 2015, he played 13 games, scored three goals, and added two assists. He would suffer through injuries in 2016 and 2017, however. After playing nine games in those two years, he bounced back to play 13 games in 2018.

It was his final season in 2019 where Seau showed exactly what he could do on the field. In 18 games, he scored 15 goals and added 10 assists, including registering a goal and two assists in a win over ACC rival Notre Dame in the NCAA Tournament quarterfinals.

"When I stepped onto campus, within a couple hours of meeting Coach [John Danowski], Matt Danowski, Coach [Ron] Caputo, and the guys that brought me around, Dave Lawson, Jake Tripucka, I knew immediately that's where I wanted to be," he said about his time at Duke. "Everyone is going to be excited Duke is calling or Coach Caputo, whoever. For me, it was a dream come true."

He originally went undrafted, but Dallas selected him in the Rookie Selection process, which was designed to reassign rookies that were drafted to the three teams (Charlotte, Florida, and Ohio) that were no longer going to compete in Major League Lacrosse in 2019.

"It's definitely exciting for sure," Seau said. "I was never expecting or playing for it. I was just playing to enjoy my time and compete with the guys at Duke. Once I got the opportunity to come here and keep playing, (being a professional athlete is) a cool experience to share with my pops. It's definitely something special. Very few people get the opportunity to do it. I'm very blessed to have the opportunity."

Seau had been putting the work in off the field. He's a self-proclaimed morning person, when he said he gets in his lifting, running, and shooting.

He credited his parents for his self-motivation and drive.

"It's just how I grew up," he said. "I grew up with my dad playing. My mom was competitive. My mom ran marathons, so it was just kind of growing up in a household of athletes, whether it's just training or competing or whatever it was. Everything was a competition, so that's how I was raised."

Seau made his MLL debut in Dallas's loss to Boston on June 9. Two weeks later against Atlanta, he was a focal point of the team's offense out of the midfield, taking eight shots and scoring a goal. He scored another goal two games later against the New York Lizards.

As Dallas dealt with a lot of roster turnover from the previous year, resulting in an 0-5 start to the season, they also had plenty of opportunities for young players like Seau to earn significant playing time, something he was extremely thankful for.

"I'm super excited to have the opportunity," he said. "Coach W, Coach Monte, and the guys have been super great working with me, just putting me in places I'll be successful. It's new playing with these guys. It's a learning curve. Each week we're getting a little bit better. The more we play with each other, the more we're able to run around and practice together. It's really exciting. It's cool to play with a new group of guys with different skill sets and keep running around.

"When I come out here and get a chance to compete and run around," he added, 'I'm going to do it as long as I can."

Seau isn't the only player with a well-known dad on the Rattlers roster, either. Another midfielder on the Rattlers is Bucknell graduate Nick Steinfeld. His dad is Jake Steinfeld, of "Body by Jake" fame; he also is one of the co-founders of Major League Lacrosse, which is how Nick was introduced to the sport while living in California.

"Watching Mark Millon, Gary Gait, those guys playing, looking up to them, seeing how good they are, striving to be like them and play in the league eventually, being on the sidelines asking for players' sticks, and then you get Ryan Powell's broken shaft on the sideline. It's still up in my room," he said. "Being able to see it at such a high level early on, and growing up in L.A., it's not really around there at all, but we got to travel to the east coast during summers and watch it. Just being a part of that was awesome. That grew my love of the game and really made it all full circle for me."

Steinfeld played lacrosse at Brentwood High School and was a three-year captain and three-year team MVP; he also was a high school All-American his senior year. Unlike top high school players, however, Steinfeld never played for a club lacrosse team. Instead, he said he would go to recruiting showcase tournaments and suit up for any team that would let him play for the weekend.

He credits the success he had in high school and his eventual time at Bucknell to the drive he saw Major League Lacrosse players display.

"My senior year [of high school] was the first time we made it to the playoffs, and it's all about the hard work," he said. "I really like looking up to those guys who played for so long and played in MLL. I looked up to them. That's how it worked. I think that was the work ethic I was going for."

Steinfeld had been a member of several teams, but he did not get much game experience. At Bucknell, he played in only eight games over four seasons. He was selected as part of Israel's 30-man roster for the 2018 Federation of International Lacrosse World Championship, which was hosted by Israel, but did not make the final 23-man roster that featured current and former MLL players like Max Adler, Max Seibald, and Ari Sussman. He opened the 2019 season on Dallas's practice squad roster.

Playing professionally had always been Steinfeld's goal, however, and he was grateful to continue to get an opportunity to be on a team, especially in the league his dad helped build.

"It's such an awesome experience being able to play in something my dad created. Not many people can get to say they do that," he said. "From watching the players at such a young age in 2001 when it first started, to seeing how it's grown, to being able to be a part of it and being one of the players that gets to keep playing the game professionally is the best experience I ever imagined."

Being so close to the league since its inception, watching its growth, knowing how hard the people involved from the field to the front office work to be a part of it and how difficult it is to get to that level, Steinfeld was disappointed when he heard people bash the league and call it a "glorified beer league."

"They just don't understand the full spectrum of it," he said. "It's such an amazing sport and an amazing league. It gives people the opportunity to keep playing after college. It's definitely not considered to be as on tier as the NFL or NBA, but it's still a professional sport. It gives people the opportunity to play after college, and for the people that do play in it, it's serious. It's a lot of fun. We all take it seriously. It's an awesome experience for everyone that's a part of it."

When the Rattlers moved to Dallas, they immediately moved into one of the nicest facilities in the league: Ford Center at The Star. The Rattlers players and staff appreciated the amenities, and the building was the envy of many visiting players around the league.

"This facility is unbelievable," Boston defender James Fahey said. "I don't think there's going to be any facilities the MLL will host games in that compare to this in regards to the amenities in the locker room and all the infrastructure surrounding this facility, including the social scene outside. Beautiful field. This turf is great. The lighting is great. The temperature, the way they run the air conditioning in here is incredible. I wouldn't mind playing every single game here. It's awesome playing in this facility."

Unfortunately, in the early parts of the 2019 season, another reason many visiting players enjoyed being at The Ford Center is because they earned a road victory.

In the July 7 game against Boston, Dallas jumped out to a 4-1 lead, but the Cannons outscored Dallas 6-1 in the second quarter and came away with a 15-11 victory; it was Dallas's sixth consecutive loss to start the season and third home loss.

"I don't think I've ever been in this situation," said Dallas midfielder Donny Moss.

Moss was born and raised in Rochester and grew up watching the Rattlers, who featured some of the best talent in the league and won the championship in 2008, the year before Moss made his debut.

"I had season tickets to the first season ever in Rochester. They played at Frontier Field, which is where the baseball team played," he said. "The teams were stacked. You had John Grant and Casey Powell. Teams were insane. The who's who of 90s lacrosse, 90s and early 2000s. It's the perfect education of the game at that level."

Moss turned pro in the summer of 2009, drafted out of Adelphi by Long Island. His hometown Rattlers had dissolved after the 2008 season, and the team was transferred to an ownership group in Toronto, where the Rattlers would become the Toronto Nationals (the team moved to Hamilton in 2011 and folded after the 2013 season).

Meanwhile, the Chicago Machine moved to Rochester in 2011 and rebranded as the Rattlers. Moss joined the Rattlers in 2014, and it had been a dream come true for him.

"It's always been a dream of mine to play for this team," said Moss. "I stayed loyal to this program and organization. These people are great. They treat me great. Coaching staff is awesome. Players are great. The fans are incredible. What else do I need?"

What Moss and the Rattlers needed were victories, but even after another game was added to the loss column in the standings, Moss remained optimistic.

"We're working things out," he said. "We've got the players to play. We've got some stud athletes. We just have to put it all together. This is all new to all of us. We'll just keep grinding, and we'll get one of these wins soon, trust me."

James Cirrone/Pretty Instant

Will Sands (22) suffered a broken hand that cut his 2018 rookie season short, but he chose to come back to MLL and the Boston Cannons in 2019 to pick up where he left off.

Brett Davis/Pretty Instant

Thanks to the removal of the MLL and NLL overlap, Randy Staats (83) and Shayne Jackson (32) finally participated in an MLL training camp. Playing for Georgia teams in the MLL and NLL, they were proud to help grow the game in Atlanta.

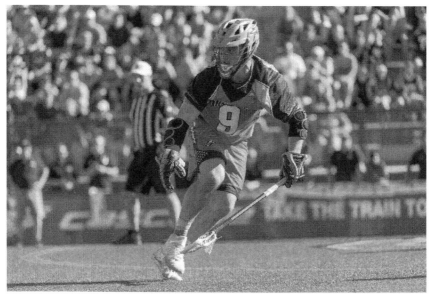

Ron Chenoy/Pretty Instant

Max Adler may have started playing lacrosse late, but the Division 2 face-off specialist went from last-round draft pick to MLL All-Star in a short amount of time.

Nick Weaver/Pretty Instant

Bryce Wasserman (2) was dedicated to the Dallas Rattlers and growing the game in his hometown. His commitment was so strong, he took a helicopter to get from a wedding to the team's game on September 7.

Donnie Riggs/Pretty Instant

Nick Mariano (23) was playing for a different team in 2019, but his uniform number – chosen to honor a deceased friend – remained the same.

Wesley Bunnell/Pretty Instant

Dylan Molloy originally wasn't going to play in Major League Lacrosse in the summer of 2019, but he was happy he changed his mind and joined the team he grew up cheering in the stands.

5.
JULY 20
NEW YORK AT CHESAPEAKE

Matt Abbott: Donnie Riggs/Pretty Instant

At a quarter past 10 A.M., it was 92 degrees outside in Annapolis, Maryland. The country – the Mid-Atlantic in particular – was in the middle of a heat wave. In the 10 days from July 11 to July 20, nine days registered at least 90 degrees, with the July 17, 18, and 19 hitting 95 degrees, 94 degrees, and 96 degrees, respectively. It was expected that July 20 would hit 98 degrees.

The Bayhawks game against the New York Lizards was pushed back from 7:00 P.M. to 8:00 P.M.

"We're in a dilemma today. Is it healthy to play today?" Bayhawks head coach Dave Cottle said. "It's going to be a 12-degree difference between 7 and 8."

To help ease the strain on the players, Cottle made that morning's walkthrough voluntary. The activity at the walkthrough was light; it included some shooting while the defenders participated in long toss.

One of the players at the walkthrough was Matt Abbott. The midfielder was in the midst of his 11th season in Major League Lacrosse. He was the longest tenured player on the team – the franchise's all-time leader in games played – and one of the longest tenured players in the entire league alongside Denver's John Grant Jr. (14 seasons), Dallas's Donny Moss (11 seasons), Boston's P.T. Ricci (11 seasons), and New York's Mike Unterstein (11 seasons).

When Abbott joined the league, MLL had just contracted from 10 teams (a league-high) to six teams (a league-low); the Los Angeles Riptide, Philadelphia Barrage, New Jersey Pride, Rochester Rattlers, and San Francisco Dragons folded, although the Rattlers staff and players transferred to a new team, the Toronto Nationals.

Fewer teams meant fewer roster opportunities, which made it harder for players to find a role and playing time. As a two-way midfielder who was capable on both offense and defense, Abbott was able to establish a role for himself from the beginning, however, and hadn't looked back.

"I love the game. I've always loved it. I want to play it for as long as possible," he said. "The draft, it was on a Wednesday night. The Bayhawks played in Denver on Saturday. All of us rookies didn't make that trip; it was too quick of a turnaround. I played in every game the rest of the year that year. To be able to find a way on the field, to try and help the team win, meant a lot."

Abbott was born into the game. His grandfather, Larry, and father, Tom, both played lacrosse at Syracuse University, one of the biggest powerhouses in college lacrosse. Even his older brother, Mike, played at the University of Virginia and Cortland State.

Growing up in Syracuse, all Abbott wanted to do was follow in his family's footsteps and play lacrosse at Syracuse. At Nottingham High School, he played lacrosse from eighth grade through his senior season and was a three-time captain.

At Syracuse, Abbott played all 64 games during his four years. He was an All-American as a junior and senior, and the Orange won national titles both those years.

Abbott said there was a difference between reaching his goal of playing at Syracuse and playing at a high level at Syracuse. As he experienced success as an upper classman, he then believed playing at a higher level was also a possibility.

"I played it my whole life," he said. "I can't imagine not playing it."

Playing in his first MLL game was an eye-opening experience.

"My first game I played against [Syracuse legend] Gary Gait," Abbott said. "I remember watching him growing up, so it was a little bit of an adjustment to get up to speed."

Syracuse is one of the collegiate programs with the most storied histories. The two championships Abbott helped the Orange win bumped the program's total number of titles to 10, the most in Division 1.

He was drafted onto another team with a strong fan base and a winning history. In the eight seasons prior to drafting Abbott, Chesapeake (which previously played as the Baltimore Bayhawks and the Washington Bayhawks before moving to Annapolis in 2009) played in four of the first five championship games, winning two of them.

From the organization's last championship in 2005 through 2008 – the team's final season before drafting Abbott – the team had not reached the playoffs, let alone the Championship Game, however. That streak continued in Abbott's rookie year, but the organization returned to dominance in the coming years. From 2010 through 2013, the team reached the playoffs every season and won three championships.

The Bayhawks only reached the playoffs once in the following five seasons (it was 2018, the most recent season), but Abbott was proud of the accomplishments he and the team have achieved.

"What we've done with the Bayhakws since then is we've won three titles during my tenure here, to give the Bayhawks five, the most in the league," he said. "I'm very grateful to be a part of a great Syracuse tradition and now a great Bayhawks tradition."

In 11 years, Abbott saw ups, like the championships, and downs, like the league contracting for a second time prior to the 2019 season.

What he was impressed by, however, was not just the growth of the talent pool in the past 11 seasons, but the growth of the fan base, especially in nontraditional hotbeds.

"The Outlaws have had great success in our league," Abbott said. "They've got a great fan base. Being there for the Fourth of July game, between 25 and 30 thousand people in the stands even after lightning delays and hailstorm delays, it's a great environment to play in. It's great to see the growth of the sport.

"The Hound Legion in Charlotte, I always enjoyed going there and playing because they had such passion for that team," he added. "It's encouraging. We're going to see more of that as time goes on and the sport continues to grow. The future of lacrosse is bright in the hotbeds as well as the nontraditional areas."

Chesapeake head coach Dave Cottle had coached Abbott for six years at the professional level. He consistently applauded his work ethic and said he is "so smart of a player." Those attributes played a large role in his ability to play in Major League Lacrosse, but Abbott also believed luck played a large role as well.

"Thankfully for me and a lot of the guys, we dedicate a lot of our free time on the weekends to make this happen," he said. "I'm thankful my work schedule still allows me to play. I'm pretty lucky injury-wise to still be playing after 10 seasons, in my 11th year. It's been fun. When I look back on it, I hope I have more years to reflect on it to come, but when I look back on the people I've met, the relationships I've made, just the good memories, it's hard to believe it's been 11 seasons and 10 years already. It's been a great ride. I hope my body and abilities can allow me to do it a little while longer."

In 2019, Abbott was selected to play in the MLL All-Star Game, scheduled for July 27 in front of the Bayhawks home fans in Annapolis, Maryland, the first time the city hosted the league's best. It was his ninth time playing in the All-Star game.

He was also hoping to win his fourth MLL title, and the Bayhawks seemed to be in a good position to contend for the championship with a 4-2 record prior to the July 20 game against the Lizards.

Long-term, however, Abbott hoped to help raise the profile of the league to make sure it was a place future generations of lacrosse stars had the opportunity to play in.

"Obviously, it's still a niche sport, in my opinion, but growing at a rapid pace in certain areas," he said. "Still, you go to a lot of places, even in this country, and they may not know what lacrosse is or be aware there is a pro league around. It's encouraging to see the growth. MLL was around pretty much throughout my middle school and high school years. That was when the league first started. There was always that opportunity, at least when I was of age, to be able to play. I hope through us giving back and trying to raise the profile of this sport can make that a possibility for the next several generations to come."

Another player at the walkthrough was midfielder Nick Mariano. While he played at Syracuse like Abbott, he did not have the years of experience in MLL or with the Bayhawks that Abbott did; he was drafted fourth overall in the 2017 draft by the Florida Launch and was acquired by the Bayhawks prior to the 2019 season in the disbursement draft when the Launch, Charlotte Hounds and Ohio Machine all folded.

He was a two-time All-American in his two years at Syracuse (he transferred from UMass after his sophomore season), and he enjoyed two seasons of 30-plus goals. Being a professional lacrosse player was something he had wanted to do since childhood.

"Growing up in [Yorktown Heights, N.Y.], there's a lot of professional lacrosse players," he said, referring to former MLL players like Brian Carcaterra, John Ranagan, and the legendary Roy Colsey. "That was one of the goals you reach for. When I was younger, I remember watching games in the summer on ESPN. It was like 20, 21 games. They were fun games to watch and something I always wanted to be in. You're in an environment with the best lacrosse players in the world, on and off the field. Not only are they great lacrosse players, they're great people. That was something I always wanted to be a part of. I'm humbled and honored to be a part of that situation now."

He also wasn't the only Mariano on the field. His older brother, Tom, was an assistant coach for the Bayhawks in 2019 and was also the head coach of the Florida Launch when Nick was drafted.

While several brothers have played together in Major League

Lacrosse like Casey, Ryan, and Mikey Powell or Chris, Matt, and Mike Bocklett, Nick and Tom are the second brother player-coach combination in the league; the other instance was when Joe Spallina coached brother Brian Spallina when the New York Lizards won the MLL championship in 2015.

"It's been awesome we can share it as a family. I don't know how many brother-player coaches there were, so it's pretty cool to be in that situation," Nick said. "It's our opportunity to play the game we love and coach the game we love so much. It's something we don't take for granted. When I went into the draft, I was ok with not being picked by them. I would've been pissed to play against them, just to get that extra chip on my shoulder, but in general, I think it's a cool situation for us."

Tom Mariano joined the league in 2013 when Bear Davis called and asked him to be an assistant on his staff with the Ohio Machine. He wasn't sure he wanted to get involved, at first, because of his collegiate coaching and recruiting responsibilities – Tom Mariano was the head coach at Pace University – as well as enjoying time with his family, but he acquiesced and is thankful he did.

In 2017, the Launch made Tom Mariano the second head coach in franchise history.

"It was a privilege and something I cherished and took advantage of every opportunity," he said. "But I look at it, whether it was as head coach or assistant, make me a ball boy or whatever, I think it's just an honor and privilege to be around these players and this league."

The Launch became an expansion franchise in time for the 2014 season, the same time the Hamilton Nationals folded. Florida assumed the Hamilton roster and coaching staff, but many did not make the trip with the team.

Florida suffered in its first three seasons, failing to make the playoffs and finishing with a three-win, last place finish in 2016.

The Mariano brothers helped turned things around, however. Alongside veteran MLL stars Austin Kaut, Tucker Durkin, Kieran McArdle, Connor Buczek, and Steven Brooks, as well as impact rookies Dylan Molloy (the first overall pick in the 2017 draft), Ryan Drenner, Sergio Salcido, and Jarrod Neumann, the Launch went 8-6 and reached the playoffs for the first time. The team even improved its average attendance by 608 fans per game.

Nick Mariano scored 16 goals in nine games as a rookie, and Tom Mariano was named MLL Coach of the Year.

Florida lost to eventual champions Ohio Machine in the semifinals, but there was a lot to be proud of.

"I think relationships I made in those two years together are going to last me a lifetime," Nick said. "That's the cool part about it; not only did we do well on the field, but we did well off the field and came together as a group. I remember sitting together in the locker room at Ohio after we lost, and we were there for an extra hour and a half because we were so tight, and we cared more about each other than lacrosse itself."

"That first year, that's a group they'll remember for the rest of their lives," Tom added. "The fact the team isn't there, it adds a lot more because at least we could accomplish that together. We'll always have that. You can't take it away from us, no matter what."

The 2019 season brought a lot of change to Major League Lacrosse. Players like Neumann, Durkin, McArdle, Brooks, and Drenner all left for the PLL. The Launch folded. The Marianos found their own ways to the Bayhawks, however, and they made their new situation work for them. The Bayhawks entered the July 20 game against the Lizards on a two-game winning streak and with a 4-2 record. It was not surprising the two found success amidst the change.

For Tom, it was all about doing the best you could with what you had at the time.

"I'm a big believer in enjoy what you're doing, live in the moment, control what you can control, be the very best you can be every day," Tom Mariano said. "I feel my job is to make every player and every team I've been associated with, I want to make every player, every team better. Everything else, that's out of my control. I'll do what I can to help. You want me to move chairs? I'll move chairs. I don't care. One thing in our family you learn is be a doer, don't be a watcher. Just go do it."

It's not just playing lacrosse at the highest level that Nick is doing as a Major League Lacrosse player, either. He's also honoring a friend.

Up until eighth grade, Nick was a water boy for the Ossining High School football team and developed a friendship with one of the players, Christian Federico. In 2007, Federico was a key player on the state sectional and regional championship winning football team, and Mariano was there to celebrate with him.

During Mariano's freshman year of high school, Federico – then a student at Maryland University – untimely passed away. In 2014, four years after his death, Ossining High School erected a memorial at Dilley Field in his honor, with his number 23 painted large on a brick wall.

Just like the school honored him with the number 23 memorial, Nick Mariano switched his jersey number to 23, and he still wears it to this day with the Bayhawks. The switch was to not only honor his friend but also to be posthumously inspired by him.

"I wear it with pride and a lot of passion," he said. "I'm very emotional and wear my emotions on my sleeve. I'm a very outward person. If I get angry or mad or upset or happy, I'll express it. I think that's why I wear that number. It gives me a little more motivation to play a little harder because I know that's what Christian was like. He always put his heart and soul on the field, and he didn't take no for an answer, which is how I try to take that mentality on and off the field. I try to carry on the great legacy he had. I may not be doing the best job at it, but I'm definitely trying to progress and get to that point."

Chesapeake goalie Niko Amato did not go to Syracuse. He was not a first-round draft pick. He didn't get introduced to the sport through older family members that played.

He was, however, a fan of the league at a very early age; he was a Philadelphia Barrage season ticket holder, and it left a large imprint on him.

"The play was incredible," Amato said. "The players were super interactive with the fans and couldn't be nicer. I had some personal relationships with some of the players growing up. They made the experience really fun for a fan because they had some tents off to the side where you could have a fastest shot competition or whatever. Having it in a small venue like Villanova or a college stadium makes it a pretty unique experience for the fans because you feel like you're right on top of the action."

As a kid, Amato received private lessons from Barrage goalie and eventual Hall of Famer Brian Dougherty. Getting to see him in action with the Barrage made the sport even more fun for him. Getting onto the field during an All-Star game and getting "Doc" and his teammates to autograph his trading cards was everything a young kid could dream of. His experience with the league made him that much more passionate for the sport.

It wasn't until he was drafted in the fourth round by the Florida Launch in the 2014 MLL Draft that Amato envisioned himself actually playing in the league.

"High school and college were so important to me in the moment. I never wanted to look past those experiences," he said. "Once my college season ended, I knew I had a home waiting for me. I said, 'I love lacrosse. I'm going to continue playing this game as long as I can.'"

Amato was on the Launch roster for one season, but he only appeared in one game. One of the few players that moved to Florida from Hamilton was All-Star goalie Brett Queener, and he earned most of the playing time in goal. In 2015, the Launch acquired fellow second-year goalie, Pennsylvania-native, and Dougherty-disciple Austin Kaut from the Boston Cannons; Queener played ten games and nearly 400 minutes in goal while Kaut served as the primary backup, making five appearances and playing just over 200 minutes.

The Bayhawks acquired Amato prior to the 2015 season, bringing him back to the state he played his college lacrosse. The change in scenery didn't result in more playing time than in his rookie season, however. For the first two seasons, Amato combined to play in five games.

"For a few years, it was tough being a backup or not seeing as much time as I would've liked," he said. "I tried to do what always made me successful at every level of lacrosse which is work hard, be a good teammate, show up, and do the work."

In 2017, Amato ended up with the most playing time between the pipes for the Bayhawks, going 5-3 in 10 games and nearly 459 minutes of action. It was in 2018, however, that Amato truly broke out. Although he started the season as the backup, veteran Brian Phipps went down with an injury in the second game of the season; Amato replaced him and remained the starter for the rest of the year, and with a 12.37 goals against average and .537 save percentage, he was named co-Goalie of the Year.

"Every level, every player steps up. They want to strive to do their best or be the best. That's true for me too," he said. "When I finally got my shot, I feel I was able to make the most of it."

The lack of playing time early in his career could have deterred him, and he has heard the complaints levied against the league in his now six-year career, but Amato didn't let any of it bother him. He was perfectly happy where he is.

"I know some people have some gripes with the league or whatever. There's definitely some ups and downs. For me personally, I feel like the MLL has been great to me the past five plus years," he said. "Outside of maybe a flight delay or waiting for my bags a little bit at baggage claim like any other person, I haven't experienced too many lows from an MLL standpoint. The journey has been really fantastic so far. It's been a great experience. I wouldn't trade it for anything else."

Amato's 2019 season was off to a solid start, and he was voted to play in his first All-Star game.

The individual awards and accolades he was racking up were nice, but Amato just wanted to push himself as an individual and help his team win a championship; he was still looking for his first title in either college or the pros.

What was most important to him as a player in Major League Lacrosse, however, was building relationships with the fans just like the players of yesteryear did with him.

"Any time there's kids that want autographs or whatever I can do to help them or hang out with them for a little bit, I try to do that as much as possible," he said. "Something going back to my college days, people show up and pay to see you play. The least we can do is spend some time with them afterwards, talk to them, and build a relationship. That's one of the cool things about the sport of lacrosse. It's not to that point of the NBA or NFL, so spending five minutes to make a kid's day really isn't all that much for us. Anyone who comes to support us, I try to support them back. That's something I take pretty serious."

One person who had seen Amato's accessibility first-hand was Joe Whittaker. He was a Bayhawks season-ticket holder who went to the games with his son, who started playing lacrosse at six-years-old.

Frequently, Whittaker's wife accompanied him and his son to the games, but he added that sometimes she will stay home, and he brings along a friend. Even though the temperature was not a friendly one, Whittaker brought his son's scout master from his son's Boy Scouts troop to the game; Whittaker said the scout master hadn't grown up playing sports, nor had he been to an MLL game, but they brought him along because he came to one of his son's games and was interested in experiencing the sport with them.

Whittaker was in the Coast Guard for nine years and also appreciated the way the team and the league salutes the military. He loved to root for his hometown team.

"They've invited us to do the St. Patrick's Day parade in Annapolis. We got to be with the players," he said. "I like having a team I can go to and root for to say, 'This team is from my hometown. This is who I'm rooting for.' I grew up as an Oakland Raiders fan because Baltimore didn't have a football team."

One of the reasons he loved coming to the Bayhawks games ws exactly what Amato was talking about: interaction with the fans, especially the kids.

"I like this because it's what football originally started out as. The players are accessible. They're friendly. After the game, you can go out and talk to them," he said. "My son is a goalie. Brian Phipps, the way he's reached back to my son, Niko, the way he's talked to my son, the way my son likes to watch the goalies, I've got autographed stuff they've given to my son."

Whittaker pulled out his phone and opened several pictures of his son's room, decorated with autographed lacrosse gear, including cleats signed by former MLL MVP Paul Rabil. He explained how he had kept a binder for his son full of every program from games they've attended, and that he started collecting the new Parkside MLL trading cards for his son. They even have a ball that came off an errant pass and hit Joe in the chest in his seats.

The memorabilia was exciting, but Whittaker said the best part of going to the games was the experience his son had.

"To see him light up and think, 'Hey, maybe one day I can be out there on the field to play,' that's one of my things for him," he said. "If he's getting enjoyment out of it, I'm getting enjoyment out of it."

Dave Cottle was the Chesapeake Bayhawks head coach, and he too was from Baltimore. He started playing lacrosse as a tenth grader at Baltimore's Northern High School.

"The one person I admired the most was the football coach, and I was a quarterback, and he said if I wanted to be the starting quarterback my junior or senior year, I had to play lacrosse," he said, "so I quit playing baseball in tenth grade and started playing lacrosse."

His entire lacrosse life had taken place in Maryland. He played at

Salisbury State, where he was a three-time All-American, and in 1975, he led the nation in scoring. He then served as a graduate assistant at Salisbury for two years.

From there, he coached at Severn School and won back-to-back Maryland Scholastic Association championships. He moved on to Loyola in 1983 and coached there through 2001. In his second season, the team went 10-4, beginning a stretch of 18-consecutive winning seasons; they finally made the NCAA Tournament in 1988, which started a streak of 14 consecutive appearances in the NCAA Tournament.

Cottle was hired to be the head coach of the University of Maryland in September of 2001 and coached there beginning with the 2002 season through the 2010 season.

When his contract at Maryland expired after the 2010 season, he received a call from Bayhawks majority owner Brendan Kelly, who headed Hometown Lacrosse, LLC, which had bought the team earlier in the year.

"He asked me if I would be a consultant for him," Cottle remembered. "It took a couple weeks, and I said, 'Sure.' It was a two-week break where the teams weren't allowed to practice, but I wasn't a coach and the players ran players only practices before they went to the playoffs."

The Bayhawks eventually won the 2010 MLL championship.

Cottle was promoted to head coach in 2012, and he remained in that position for four years, helping the organization win two more championships. He retired after the 2015 season and became the team's general manager, but he returned to the sidelines to coach the Bayhawks in 2018, helping to lead them back to the playoffs after a four-year drought.

Staying with the Bayhawks and returning to coach were easy decisions for Cottle.

"That starts with the owner. Brendan Kelly offered me a job and wants to build it where I live and has invested a ton of money in this," he said. "I just have decided that's probably a little more important for me than anything else."

Tom Mariano interviewed for the Bayhawks head coaching position made vacant by Cottle's absence in 2016; he did not get the job (that went to Brian Reese, who had both played for the Bayhawks and was an assistant coach under Cottle), but the organization was impressed with him and brought him in as an assistant coach.

Mariano was hired away from the Bayhawks after one season to become the head coach of the Launch. When Florida folded, however, and Cottle had a chance to bring Mariano back to Annapolis, he did so.

In addition to their positive relationship, the two had very similar philosophies concerning coaching: it was all about the relationships they made with the players.

"I get a chance to sit down with [the players] in a hotel, talking with players about their future families and they want to have kids, or they have kids, and young kids getting jobs, and watching guys grow from young pros to adults. I cherish and relish every second of this," Mariano said. "I have relationships with guys I coached in 2013 that I haven't coached in five years.

"In the MLL, it's not just about the playing," he added. "When you're playing at a high level, sometimes you win, sometimes you lose. It's how you treat them."

Cottle is one of the most respected figures in the sport, especially in Major League Lacrosse. A big reason for that is the relationship he formed with players, even those that weren't on his team.

"I learned as I got older that the players were the most important commodity in the game, and that we had to do a better job of treating the players," he said. "I love the players. I love the sacrifices they make to play in this league. I love their competitive spirit, and to me, the only reason I'm still coaching in this league is because of how much joy it is to be in a locker room with a group of guys who are all down for a common goal."

Those relationships are also what made the 2019 season, where several players left for the PLL, a challenging one for him.

"I cared so much about the guys that were on our team last year, and it broke my heart that they're no longer here," Cottle said. "How do I treat them? I'm just going to treat them the way I always treated them, but it hurt us, and it hurt the Bayhawks to lose some guys, but the ones that stayed, we got to build a much better relationship with because through tough times, they wound up being around. Colin Heacock and those guys, and for Lyle [Thompson] to stick it out, and Steele [Stanwick], now you're able to take your relationship to the next level.

"I don't blame [the guys that left for the PLL] for doing whatever was best for them," Cottle said, "because some guys were at the end of their career. They needed to go for the money. Other guys were young guys who decided maybe I can make this professional lacrosse thing work. But that was the most difficult. What you do is you submerge yourself in your team and try to get them better."

Cottle also had ideas for how the league could improve, getting more attention and bringing in more money for the players.

"I like the idea of this league ending on Labor Day weekend. With a three-day weekend, the players don't mind playing multiple games in a week, and with that, you have multiple practices, and with multiple practices, you have improved performances," he said. "I like the June start. I'd like a September ending and then maybe traveling shows with the players where they make additional money for the guys that aren't coaches or aren't teachers and then make additional money in the fall and winter traveling to other places that we may be able to encourage somebody to buy a franchise."

On July 20, Chesapeake was not the better team. New York won the game 14-10, but the score was not indicative of the dominance New York displayed. The Lizards went into the final quarter with a 13-7 lead. It took two goals in the final 15 seconds to get the Bayhawks to even score in double digits.

Ben Randall, a first-time All-Star defenseman with the Lizards, held Lyle Thompson – who, coming into the night, was averaging six points a game – to two goals and one assist; one of Thompson's goals came while Randall was off the field, serving a penalty.

"Honestly, the flow of the game never got to where we wanted it to," an exhausted Thompson said. "I think between the lines is where we really struggled. Our one-on-one matchups, I think, we lost, and we never got into all our offensive schemes and systems. It was tough to get in the flow of things."

Still, Cottle was optimistic about the future of his team; after all, they did have 10 players in the MLL All-Star Game the following week, the most of any other team.

It wasn't just his team he hoped would have brighter days ahead, however.

"This league has so much potential to be great," Cottle said. "I just hope someday we hit our potential."

6.
JULY 27
MLL ALL-STAR GAME

Isaiah Davis-Allen: Ron Chenoy/Pretty Instant

According to the Maryland Office of Tourism's website, lacrosse is the state's official state team sport. It was designated as such in 2004, 42 years after jousting became the official sport of Maryland. The state is where the sport's Hall of Fame is located, and it is home to three colleges (Maryland, Johns Hopkins, and Loyola) that combined to win 13 men's national championships from 1971 through 2019. The University of Maryland also won 14 women's national championships since 1982, the most of any other program and, in 2019, double the number of the school in second place (Northwestern, with seven).

The NCAA was founded in 1906, but it didn't begin hosting an annual men's lacrosse tournament to determine the national championship until 1971. Prior to then, the United States Intercollegiate Lacrosse Association awarded gold medals to the teams with the best records from 1926 through 1935, and then it issued the Wingate Memorial Trophy to the program with the top record from 1936 to 1970.

The Naval Academy, located in Annapolis, Maryland, was named champion or co-champion 17 different times from 1928 through 1970.

It's no surprise that when Major League Lacrosse was founded in 2001, one of the teams was placed in Maryland. The Bayhawks originally played home games in Baltimore, bouncing between Homewood Field at Johns Hopkins, M & T Bank Stadium (the home field of the Baltimore Ravens), and Johnny Unitas Stadium at Towson University. In 2007, the Bayhawks split home games between George Mason University in Virginia and Georgetown in Washington, D.C. The following season, the team played at George Mason University and one game at the Navy-Marine Corps Memorial Stadium in Annapolis. Finally, in 2009, the team announced a three-year deal to continue playing at the Navy-Marine Corps Memorial Stadium, and it's where the team had played ever since (the team did have a proposal in 2017 to build a new stadium in Anne Arundel County, but it had not moved forward as of the summer of 2019).

Despite the rich lacrosse history in Maryland, only once, in 2002, had the league played its All-Star Game in the state of Maryland. It was a big deal, therefore, when the league announced in 2018 that the following summer, the All-Star Game would be hosted by the Chesapeake Bayhawks in Annapolis, Maryland.

"It's an honor and pleasure for the Bayhawks organization to be recognized by the League and Commissioner Sandy Brown for our outstanding game day presentation," Bayhawks President Mark Burdett said in a press release at the time. "We have always worked extremely hard to give our fans the best access, energy and competition when they commit their time and treasure to support our team. We will replicate and even strive to improve the great entertainment the best in lacrosse can provide."

While the Navy-Marine Corps Memorial Stadium may not have been as large as Empower Field at Mile High, home to the Denver Outlaws and the NFL's Denver Broncos, or as new and sleek as Ford Center at The Star, where the Dallas Rattlers play, but it was a special place to play for Bayhawks players, even for the ones that were from Canada.

"You look around at all the battles, and you realize the sacrifices people have gone through," said Chesapeake midfielder John Wagner, "not only for Americans, but for Canadians to play this game of lacrosse every weekend and for us to be flown out around the country and across borders. You can look up in the sky and be thankful. I am grateful to play at Navy Stadium."

Two weeks before the All-Star Game in Annapolis, Chesapeake's Lyle Thompson and New York's Rob Pannell, two of the game's most recognizable stars, were named as the two team captains and were responsible for selecting the rosters for the game from a pool of players fans voted in, including Atlanta's Tommy Palasek and Chris Madalon, Boston's Nick Marrocco and James Fahey, Chesapeake's Matt Abbott and Nick Mariano, Dallas's Bryce Wasserman, and Denver's Max Adler.

One week before the All-Star Game, fans in Annapolis got a little preview of the exhibition as Thompson, Chesapeake, and 10 other Bayhawks selected as All-Stars took on Pannell, New York, and five other All-Stars in a regular season game.

Isaiah Davis-Allen, a midfielder with the Bayhawks, was chosen to be on Thompson's team, Team Ice. From Springfield, Virginia, Davis-Allen played collegiately at the University of Maryland and was selected in the second round (16th overall) of the 2017 MLL Collegiate Draft. Earning a trip to his second consecutive MLL All-Star Game, Davis-Allen was excited to represent his home team in his adopted state.

"For me, yes, I grew up in Virginia, but I consider myself a Maryland guy," he said. "I've settled in Fell's Point, Baltimore. I feel Maryland is doing something right. To play in front of my home crowd, the crowd I live in, is incredible. It's special playing this All-Star Game at home."

Davis-Allen said he was a hockey player growing up, but a friend talked to him about playing lacrosse. He said baseball was "getting boring," and he already had some family ties to the game as his uncle, Maurice Davis, played at Rutgers in 1981.

He committed to play at Maryland while playing for St. Stephens/St. Agnes, but the final two seasons featured some very low points in his life. According to a *Washington Post* article by Eric Detweiler from 2013, Davis-Allen broke his leg in an April practice in his junior year, ending his season. The following year, days before he graduated, his mother passed away from cancer. In another *Washington Post* article from 2014 by Roman Stubbs, Davis-Allen said the family atmosphere at Maryland helped him deal with his loss, as well as putting his energy into his college experience and spending time with his teammates.

In his final season at Maryland, he helped the team win the national championship, its first since 1975. The day before the championship game, Davis-Allen and Maryland teammates (and eventual 2019 MLL All-Stars) Colin Heacock and Nick Manis were all drafted by the Bayhawks.

Playing alongside former teammates (goalie Niko Amato was a senior in Davis-Allen's rookie year, and he also played alongside LSM Greg Danseglio) helped Davis-Allen make a smooth transition to the pro game, but he did say his mindset has shifted slightly since playing in college.

"It's pro lacrosse, and you're playing for your livelihood more," he said. "You want to prove what they're giving you is what you're worth."

Walking on the concourse at Navy-Marine Corps Memorial Stadium, it was evident that Davis-Allen was one of the more popular players in the league. His Bayhawks jersey was available for sale and his picture was on the box of Parkside Collectible MLL trading cards, a set in which he was the first card.

What was unexpected about the popularity of Davis-Allen is that he plays a position, defensive midfield, that is not glamorous and doesn't produce gaudy statistics. It's a position where, if your name is repeated multiple times, it's likely because you didn't do a good job.

It was a delight for Davis-Allen to transcend the position.

"I think it's real special," he said. "To do a comparison from our sport to football, we're the lock-down corner now. [We were like] safety or O-linemen, guys that don't get a ton of credit."

Davis-Allen was focused on performing for his team, however, he was also involved in other endeavors outside of the league. He was a general contractor and project engineer in the Baltimore area, working a nine-to-five job. He also coached lacrosse in the inner city, particularly Prince George's County.

"I coach in the untraditional areas," he said. "I focus on diversity, trying to spread the game of lacrosse in Prince George's County and with Nation United. I think it's important to have someone who looks like me playing on the field."

Growing up, Davis-Allen viewed other African-American lacrosse players like Kyle Harrison, Jovan Miller, Hakeem Lecky, and Pat Young as influences in his career, and he hoped to do the same for the players he coaches.

"I would say, traditionally, lacrosse has been a Caucasian upper middle-class sport," he said. "A lot of people are trying to change that and see it grow. ... I do it through Prince George's County. As far as race and socio economic, there's a lot of people spearheading it, and I'm one piece in the big machine."

Davis-Allen was just one of a group of standout defensive midfielders on the Chesapeake Bayhawks. Head coach Dave Cottle routinely talked about how integral the group was to the team's success. When the All-Star rosters were announced, Cottle sent a tweet congratulating all the selected players, but he also added one who he felt did not get the recognition he deserved: defensive midfielder Nick Manis.

"Just wanted to say congrats to the players who will be participating in Mll all star game. One player who didn't make the all star game from the Bayhawks is Nick Manis. I think every player on our team would tell you how respected and how valuable Nick is to our team," Cottle tweeted.

To Cottle's pleasure, Manis was added as an injury replacement for Denver's Mikie Schlosser. Not only did it mean a lot for Manis to earn the honor of being a league All-Star, it was particularly special that the game was being played in his hometown of Annapolis.

"It means everything," he said. "Having this opportunity, going from a kid who grew up here and going to these games, watching the Bayhawks play, now being someone who is actually on the field and can kind of impact the next generation, I think it is something I would never have dreamed of."

Manis's roots run deep in Maryland. His grandfather, George, played basketball for the Terrapins from 1950 through 1953, and his father, Nick, played lacrosse at Maryland from 1976 through 1980. His mother and sister also played lacrosse.

He said growing up in Annapolis helped expedite his love for the sport.

"Growing up in Annapolis, everybody plays lacrosse it feels like," he said. "I started up at a young age and went from there."

He also went to a number of Bayhawks games.

"Being able to go to games as a kid was awesome," he said. "It was the pinnacle of lacrosse. It was the best players in the world. That was something I always enjoyed going out and watching."

A three-sport athlete at Severn School, Manis was the captain and MVP for the lacrosse, football, and basketball teams. He was a two-time all-county selection in lacrosse. He was not highly recruited out of high school, but he was confident he could play at the next level; eventually, he followed in his father's footsteps to play for Maryland.

Manis was a two-way midfielder in high school, but as a freshman at the University of Maryland, head coach John Tillman and defensive coordinator Kevin Conry asked him about focusing solely on the defensive end.

After earning regular playing time as a sophomore, Manis broke his foot and missed his junior season. He came back strong as a redshirt junior, however, and was named captain the following year as a senior when Maryland won the national championship. Still, playing a position where statistics – goals, in particular – are not gaudy and Davis-Allen took his fair share of playing-time caused Manis to go overlooked.

He was selected in the eighth-round of the MLL Collegiate Draft and played in four games as a rookie, picking up two ground balls. He became a regular in 2018, however, playing in all 14 games and helping Chesapeake earn its first playoff appearance in five seasons.

Even though the defensive midfield position can be one of anonymity – a big reason why he struggled to get All-Star Game votes

– the lack of notoriety did not bother him much at all.

"I think a lot of that comes down to how you're raised," he said. "My parents have been awesome. They always told me your attitude and effort is what you can control every day. Coming out there, it doesn't matter what position you play or what role you have in your job, your company, or school, or whatever it may be; you're supposed to do a good job. You're supposed to do your best job, and I get to play with the best lacrosse players in the world in my hometown. I would play any position. I think being able to do that is awesome. I love it."

Manis wasn't the only All-Star representing Annapolis, either. Atlanta Blaze rookie face-off specialist Alex Woodall was voted to play in the All-Star Game in his first season.

Woodall played high school lacrosse at St. Mary's in Annapolis and was coached by former Bayhawks attackman (and eventual Boston Cannons assistant head coach) Ben Rubeor. He moved on to play one season at High Point University, winning .528 of his face-offs, but transferred back to the state of Maryland to play at Towson the following year. His face-off winning percentage increased every season, topping off at .742 (second-best in the nation) as a senior and helping him earn USILA Second-Team All-America honors.

The Ohio Machine used the first overall pick in the 2019 MLL Collegiate Draft to select Woodall, making him the second face-off specialist to be selected first overall behind Trevor Baptiste, who the Cannons selected with the first pick in the 2018 MLL Collegiate Draft. Roughly a month and a half later, the Premier Lacrosse League held its inaugural collegiate draft, and Woodall was selected fourth overall. When Ohio ceased operations, Woodall was picked by the Atlanta Blaze in a special draft for players entering the league out of college who either were selected by teams that folded or who were not selected at all.

Despite the twists and turns the MLL offseason endured, Woodall still signed to play for the Blaze and Major League Lacrosse.

A lot of expectations are placed on the first overall draft pick, but Woodall was earning his place in the league. He was happy to voted in as an All-Star despite only having nine professional games under his belt.

"It means a lot," he said. "It's something everyone wishes they could do growing up. Hopefully I can continue to have some success in my career and have a long one. I'm having a blast doing it."

Brian Phipps, another professional player from Annapolis, wasn't even playing in the All-Star Game, but it was still important for him to be there.

A veteran in his ninth season and in his second stint with the Bayhawks, Phipps spent most of the first half of the season backing up Niko Amato. Still, he was at the All-Star Game in his hometown in order to coach a pregame clinic.

"This is one of the best venues for lacrosse in the country," he said. "That's really cool to have the best players in the world playing in my hometown and showcasing their skills in front of our hometown fans and friends and just putting their lacrosse on the map."

Like Manis, Phipps was from a Maryland lacrosse family. His grandfather, Louis, his father, Wilson, and his brother, Michael, all played for Maryland before him. Also, while she wasn't a Terp, Phipps's mother, Betty, played lacrosse and field hockey at Roanoke. Even now, his wife, formerly Caitlyn McFadden, is a former Tewaaraton Award winner from the University of Maryland and an assistant coach for the school's women's lacrosse team.

Phipps remembered going to Bayhawks games as a child and then again in his senior season before he was drafted by the Bayhawks in the 2010 supplemental draft. He played 10 games as a rookie and was named an All-Star that season, the first of three eventual selections.

In addition to playing goalie on the weekends in summer, Phipps was a history teacher and boys' lacrosse coach at Archbishop Spalding High School in Severn, Maryland. He said being a professional athlete (Phipps said he always wanted to be a professional but acknowledged he was not the biggest, fastest or strongest, so "the football and basketball dreams I had were not there,") impressed his students.

"Some kids are like, 'Oh, Coach Phipps, you have a Wikipedia page,' or, 'I saw your highlights on YouTube,'" he said. "This day and age, it's pretty cool to have that experience, and those kids I'm teaching are freshmen and sophomores. They've seen me play for the last five, ten years. It's pretty cool to have that following and backing. It gives me street cred in the classroom as well."

There are a number of reasons goalie is a challenging position, but the one facing Phipps was that only one goalie can play on the field at a time. Despite three previous All-Star selections and eight seasons of experience, Phipps was in a new role as a backup. He returned to the

Bayhawks in 2017 after four seasons with the Ohio Machine, but in the 2018 season, he suffered an injury after five games and missed the remainder of the season. In his absence, Amato developed into one of the top goaltenders in the league, earning co-Goaltender of the Year honors. Amato continued to hold the number one goaltender job in 2019 and earned his first trip to the All-Star Game.

Phipps was not bitter, however. According to a June 2019 Capital Gazette piece written by Katherine Fominykh, he spent most of the first half of the season making himself a presence in the community, helping the Bayhawks coach clinics, visiting children's hospitals, driving the Harbor Queen before the team's Chesapeake Celebration, and visiting the Smithsonian's National Museum of the American Indian to help promote the team's upcoming Native American Celebration Night.

While he wanted to be on the field, Phipps was grateful for the opportunity to still be playing in Major League Lacrosse and with his hometown Bayhawks.

"The MLL is the first league to put professional lacrosse on the map," he said. "They've done a good job of helping us grow as professionals, as athletes, lacrosse in general. I'm very indebted to them for giving me a shot, giving me a chance, and I'm very fortunate to see where they're going and see where the game can go with the MLL backing and owners, like Brendan Kelly, who put everything into it and treat the players like royalty and treat us like professional athletes.

"It's really cool to be the hometown kid playing back for my team," he added, and "still playing for them in year 10 is pretty impressive."

While the annual All-Star Game is a way to celebrate the best in the game today, the league used the 2019 contest to also honor some legends from the past.

Former MLL players Spencer Ford and Paul Cantabene joined head coach B.J. O'Hara on the coaching staff for Team Fire while MLL alumnus and former Bayhawks head coach Brian Reese joined Bill Warder's staff on Team Ice.

"Spencer Ford and Tom Mariano reached out to me," Reese said. "They said they were looking to do some alumni people coming back for the game, so they mentioned me, and I'm free this weekend, so I jumped all over it."

While there were a number of negative developments prior to the 2019 MLL season, one of the positives the league put in place was making Ford the Special Assistant to the Commissioner for Alumni Development.

The league hosted a dinner for alumni and held its annual MLL Legends Game at the famous Lake Placid Summit Classic. Bringing back a few legends for the game helped connect the league's past to its present, and Reese and Cantabene were excited to take part.

"I thought it was a really cool thing to do since I got to play in one of the first ones," Cantabene said, "and to help out a little bit in this scenario is a special thing and see where these guys have come from to where we've come from."

Cantabene played six seasons in Major League Lacrosse, including the inaugural season, and brought home a lot of hardware in his half-dozen seasons. He won three MLL championships, was named an All-Star five times, and he was an All-MLL selection twice. When he retired, he held the league records for career face-off wins (1,015) and career ground balls (538).

While playing Major League Lacrosse, the former Loyola Greyhound accepted a job as the head men's lacrosse coach at Stevenson University, where he had been for 15 years. He also became the school's Associate Athletic Director.

When Ford and Major League Lacrosse called to offer him the opportunity to guest coach at the All-Star Game, Cantabene said he immediately accepted. He was excited to help as well as see so much lacrosse talent up close, like John Grant Jr. – someone he's played against – and Alex Woodall, a local player that played the position he loved.

Woodall, the number one draft pick, began his professional career right out of college, and it made Cantabene think about how timing is sometimes everything.

"I think these guys are doing the right thing, playing the game they love," he said. "I wish I was 21 to be able to do that. The first year of the league, I was 31. It was a little bit different."

It wasn't long ago Cantabene was on an MLL sideline. In 2017, Brian Reese, then the head coach for the Bayhawks, named Cantabene his offensive coordinator. The Bayhawks led the league in scoring that year with 211 goals, the only team to score 200 goals for the season (Denver was second with 199).

Like Cantabene, Reese did not have a long playing career in MLL, but it was very successful. In five seasons, including the inaugural season, Reese was an All-Star four times. From 2006 through 2011, Reese served as the general manager of Denver Outlaws while also coaching the team from the fifth game of the 2007 season through his resignation in 2011, winning the 2009 Coach of the Year award and boasting a four-year record of 30-12. He became the general manager of the Bayhawks in 2011, helping put together the roster that won back-to-back championships in 2012 and 2013. In 2016, he was named the team's head coach, filling in for the (briefly) retired Dave Cottle.

Since he left the Bayhawk sidelines after the 2017 season, Reese continued coaching the girls' lacrosse team at Glenelg Country School. He also spent more time with his family, including his wife, Cathy, the iconic women's lacrosse coach at the University of Maryland.

While he was brought back to help coach the All-Stars, Reese really was happy to take the role to have the best seat in the house.

"To see guys like Rob Pannell, Lyle Thompson, John Grant Jr., I played against Junior. I played with him a little bit. I coached Lyle," he said. "To see them on the same field and same offense, every time you step on the field, you see something new and different from those guys. I think that should be worth the price of admission."

Lyle Thompson and John Grant Jr. were players that captured every lacrosse fan's imagination. Their wizardry with the lacrosse stick often left defenders baffled and goalies in shock. They filled up the highlight reels not only with their goals but also with their passes.

Along with Thompson and Grant Jr., Team Ice truly cornered the market on number one attackmen from the league; Chesapeake's Colin Heacock and Dallas's Bryce Wasserman joined the fray.

It was then no surprise the first goal of the game was scored by number 24 on Team Ice. What was surprising was the 44-year-old John Grant Jr., playing in his 14th season in Major League Lacrosse, wasn't the one who scored said goal; the first goal of the 2019 MLL All-Star Game was scored by rookie Brendan Sunday, 11 weeks from playing in his final game at Towson.

"It was funny. We talked about it in the locker room," Sunday said about how he and Grant Jr. wore the same number. "He looked down at me. I looked down at him. I was like, 'You've got my number,' and he was like, 'No, you've got my number.

"He's one of the best ever to do it," he continued. 'It's amazing he's still doing it at this age. You have to respect everything he does. It was an honor to play with him tonight, and I look forward to playing against him again at some point later this season."

Sunday's goal was followed by one from Team Ice face-off specialist Max Adler. It was one of three goals from the four face-off specialists (Team Ice's Kevin Resiman (Boston) and Team Fire's Woodall scored the others).

While Team Ice held a 21-13 edge in face-off victories, Woodall said the competition was even amongst all the specialists.

"All the face off guys, there's four of us, got our fair share of face-off wins," Woodall said., "so all in all, it was a great night. It was a great turnout."

Even though Team Ice scored the first two goals of the game, Team Fire came back, outscoring Team Ice 11-7 in the second and third periods, taking a 14-11 lead going into the fourth quarter.

In the fourth quarter, however, Team Ice outscored Team Fire 4-1 to tie the game. The equalizer came from Bryce Wasserman with 1:18 remaining. Then in overtime, it was Sunday who played the hero, scoring the game-winner – his fourth goal of the night – off an assist from Thompson.

"I had some success earlier in the game sneaking from X to the backside pipe," Sunday said. "Lyle Thompson and Brendan Bomberry were running a two-man game up top. Lyle garners so much attention, so they were looking to slide early. I saw my guy fill in as the second slide. I snuck in right behind him. Lyle had the vision, one of the best visions in the world, and he found me on the backside. I was fortunate to get the finish."

Sunday also had an assist in the game, giving him five points on the night, but it was Team Fire's Dylan Molloy who was named MVP after he scored five goals and added one assist.

Sunday wasn't expecting to be the MVP, though; he never even thought he'd be playing at this level. The All-Star Game, however, cemented his place as a promising prospect in Major League Lacrosse, and it was a humbling experience.

"I grew up watching some of these guys play, like John Grant Jr. and Lyle," he said. "It's a cool experience being on the same field as them. I'll remember it for a while that's for sure."

7.
SEPTEMBER 21
ATLANTA AT NEW YORK

Austin Kaut: Wesley Bunnell/Pretty Instant

On September 21, the Premier Lacrosse League concluded its inaugural season with a championship game in Philadelphia, Pennsylvania between the Whipsnakes Lacrosse Club and Redwoods Lacrosse Club.

When initial rosters were rolled out, one player on the Redwoods roster was former Tewaaraton Award winner Dylan Molloy. On April 30, however, about one month before the start of the season, Molloy was released from the Redwoods. Josh Sims, the PLL's Head of Lacrosse, tweeted, "After serious consideration with Nat St Laurent and his staff, the Redwoods Lacrosse Club, has decided to release Dylan Molloy due to his inability to make training camp and commit to our regular season schedule. We wish him the best."

Roughly one week later, Molloy re-signed with Major League Lacrosse, and the Setauket, N.Y.-native joined his hometown New York Lizards. The move did not pay off for Molloy in the standings, as the Lizards went into the final game of the regular season having clinched the worst record in the league. Still, Molloy said he was happy with his decision.

"I had a good history with the coaches I played for and people I met along the way," he said. "Being drafted first overall, there's a lot of people being nice to me, taking care of me, so I felt like I owed them that. Getting the chance to come back to Long Island, which I never saw, was an awesome opportunity because my friends, my family, and where I work in New York City, it made the most sense for me at the time. I couldn't be happier."

Wearing a Lizards uniform was a treat for Molloy, who grew up a fan of the team and went to games with his family.

"I still have a hat signed by a bunch of the guys on the team at the time," he said. "You can't read any of the names, but [former MLL MVP] Greg Cattrano and all those guys [were there]."

Molloy was drafted with the first overall pick in the 2017 MLL Collegiate Draft by the Florida Launch after a four-year career at Brown University, where he was a two-time All-American and won the Tewaaraton Award as a junior, the same year he led Brown to the Final Four on a broken foot.

He continued to make an immediate impact at the professional level, scoring 21 goals and adding six assists in eight games as a rookie while helping lead the Florida Launch to its first playoff appearance in its short existence.

In addition to playing lacrosse professionally, the Ivy-League graduate Molloy worked during the week as an underwriter for Chubb Insurance. In a 2018 article in the Providence Journal by Kevin McNamara, Molloy said he brought his lacrosse gear to work with him every Friday, so he was prepared to travel to that week's game.

Molloy might have been balancing a busy career with professional lacrosse, but he didn't see the time spent in Major League Lacrosse as a sacrifice. He saw it as something he couldn't live without.

"It's not a sacrifice," he said. "This is the game you grew up playing. I've always had a stick in my hand. I don't know what it would be like to not be preparing for a season, honestly, so I think that comes into play for a lot of us. Coming around to the spring and not having the fresh air and getting ready for lacrosse would be a weird life to live. It's a good outlet for us. It's fun. It's an escape to have a reason to go to the wall, be on your own, get that workout in. It keeps you in shape. It's an awesome environment especially here on Long Island. MLL is doing great things. It's great to be a part of. I would like to play as long as I can."

The Lizards may not have put together the win total that everyone expected, but Molloy still put together some positive moments for his team. In 12 games prior to the season finale, Molloy was second on the team with 37 points on 24 goals and 13 assists. He was named the MLL All-Star Game MVP, and he routinely made highlights thanks to his physical style of play, running through opponents numerous times during the season. On one particular play earlier in the season against the Boston Cannons, Molloy chased a ground ball into the corner, knocked the ball through the Cannons player's legs hockey-style back towards the field, picked up the ground ball, lowered his shoulder and knocked the sliding midfielder onto his rear, got pushed from behind and bounced off a third Boston defender, switched hands, shot, and scored; it landed him in the second spot on that day's SportsCenter Top Plays.

All things considered, Molloy was happy to be playing for the Lizards, only 40 miles from his hometown.

"Playing here, I played twice in the two years I was in the league before here," he said. "Coming back from training camp felt like I was driving to high school practice. It brought back a lot of good memories with family coming and all my local friends and whatnot. It means a lot to me. It was a great decision, on my end, to come back here."

Having a strong dodger like Dylan Molloy also meant Rob Pannell, another Tewaaraton Award winner and first overall pick, had to play a different role than the dodging one he was accustomed to, but he said it was important to let Molloy do what he does.

Pannell and Molloy had a lot in common aside from being Lizards teammates. Both won college lacrosse's award for being the best player, both were the top pick in the MLL Collegiate Draft, both were strong dodgers, and both went to Ivy League schools. Additionally, both were from Long Island and grew up watching the Lizards play.

Pannell said going to Lizards games inspired him to be the best lacrosse player he could be and want to play in Major League Lacrosse one day.

"I wanted to be around the best lacrosse there was," he said. "There's no better lacrosse than the guys that are playing professionally and playing at the highest level. I dreamed to play for the Lizards. Did I actually think it was going to happen? I don't know. I continued to work hard. After having some success in high school and in college, I thought that maybe my dream could become a reality of being a professional lacrosse player and, more specifically, playing for the New York Lizards, where I've been for seven years now.

"I remember going with my dad and my brother [former Lizards teammate James Pannell], and we were really into lacrosse," he added. "My dad didn't play, but he loved the sport and made sure we were watching and getting better, and I think that's an important thing. Some of my greatest memories were going to the games with my family."

Pannell was taken first overall by the Lizards in 2012, a down time in the franchise; in addition to having one of the league's worst records the year prior, several players had asked to be traded. Making matters worse, Pannell wouldn't play in the league for another year; he had suffered an injury in his senior season and was awarded a redshirt year, giving him an extra year of eligibility. Beyond all odds and expectations, New York made the playoffs in 2012, meaning Pannell joined a better team the following year. In 2013, Pannell won the Rookie of the Year award.

Pannell helped lead the Lizards into the playoffs in four of the next five seasons, including 2015 when New York made a blockbuster trade with the Boston Cannons to acquire Paul Rabil; New York won the league championship that season. Pannell would win two Offensive

Player of the Year awards, set the record for points in a season two separate times, and win the 2018 MLL MVP award.

He was proud of what he had accomplished and was grateful to be able to do it all in front of his family, friends, and hometown fans.

"For me, it's always been about playing the sport at the highest level. I always took pride in Long Island being the hotbed of lacrosse," he said. "Being here for seven years, it's been cool to call Hofstra my home and play here with the New York Lizards."

Being from New York is something Pannell and Molloy take pride in, and the final home game of the 2019 season was also a way for them to honor other important New Yorkers. The regular season finale was the organization's "Salute to Heroes" night, honoring local military and first responders. The team was supposed to wear special camouflage print uniforms with stars and stripes in the numbers, but the uniforms, unfortunately, got lost in the mail and didn't make it in time for the game.

Still, the term "first responders" took special meaning in New York, especially ten days after the anniversary of 9/11. Molloy and Pannell were proud to be a part of what they considered just a small token of appreciation.

"It's a little offering, but I hope we have a lot of people in the stands thanking everyone that comes," Molloy said. "It means a lot to be involved, but I hope it goes a long way for those first responders and the heroes out there."

Honoring service members and first responders from New York in September had Pannell – who was in fifth grade at the time – remembering how he took in that day of infamy.

"I was young. I didn't even know what the World Trade Center was," he said. "I knew the Twin Towers, but I didn't know what went on in there and who was in there.

"To hear about and have guys like [Cornell lacrosse alumnus and Cantor Fitzgerald worker] Eamon McEneaney have such an impact on me, it means a lot more now than it did back then because I didn't know what was going on," Pannell added. "Now, to lose guys I idolized and know that was why I never had the opportunity to meet this guy everyone talks so highly about among thousands of others, it certainly makes you think back about how lucky you are and everything you have. It's great we're able to, through the sport of lacrosse, honor our heroes."

Molloy wasn't the only player to unexpectedly join the New York roster prior to the start of the season. The Lizards were able to acquire All-Stars Kevin Crowley and Austin Kaut in the dispersal draft once the Charlotte Hounds, Florida Launch, and Ohio Machine ceased operations heading into the 2019 season.

Like Pannell and Molloy, Crowley was also a first overall draft pick, taken by the Hamilton Nationals out of Stony Brook University (about 37 miles east of Hofstra, where the Lizards play) first overall in the 2011 MLL Collegiate Draft.

"It was quite a culture shock, quite a change from coming from the west coast of British Columbia to New York," said Crowley. "I had a great four years at Stony Brook. The people here are great on the island, which is one of the reasons why I wanted to become a Lizard."

Crowley started playing box lacrosse at five-years-old because his grandfather played lacrosse, and he said that's what kids in New Westminster did. He said it wasn't until he was 10-years-old that he started playing field lacrosse.

He enjoyed playing both versions of lacrosse, even if it had to be done in adverse situations.

"We were indoors in the summers and outdoors in the winters, however backwards that was," he said. "I remember there were some cold games, and they didn't do weather delays. You were playing in snow or freezing rain. That sticks out in my mind of funny memories. You didn't know any different, so you just did it. It might've been miserable, but it was fun."

Crowley wasn't just taken first in the MLL draft; he was also drafted first by the Philadelphia Wings in the 2012 NLL Entry Draft, the first player to be selected first in both leagues (Lyle Thompson eventually joined him in this elusive club when he was drafted first overall by the MLL's Florida Launch and NLL's Georgia Swarm in 2015).

Crowley said to be the first player selected with the top pick in both leagues was "cool," but he also said there's so many talented players available in the drafts that being selected first was a "crapshoot." What he had more control over, however, was how he won the MLL MVP award in 2013, just his third in the league. That season, Crowley scored 38 goals, including three two-point scores, and added 14 assists, and the Hamilton Nationals lost by one goal in the semifinals to the eventual champions, the Chesapeake Bayhawks.

Still, he passed the credit for that season on to those around him for the success he enjoyed.

"That was a lot of fun," he said. "Dave Huntley was our coach. I love Hunts, rest in peace. He's one of my favorite coaches I ever had. I had a great relationship with him. We had a great team. We had Joe Walters, Brodie Merrill. Brett Queener was in goal. We had a lot of great pieces. Dave Huntley did a great job of putting me in a place where I could be successful, and the guys around me were great lacrosse players drawing a lot of attention."

The fun didn't last long, however. That season was the final one the Nationals played in Canada before folding and the players and coaching staff were moved to Florida. Crowley played eight games for the Launch before they traded him to the Bayhawks in a deal at the trade deadline. He played one more season in Chesapeake before joining the Charlotte Hounds in 2016.

Although the Hounds were one of the newest teams in the league, founded in 2012 alongside the Ohio Machine, Charlotte was home to one of the more well-known fan groups in Major League Lacrosse, Hound Legion. Even when the fans lost their team, Hound Legion was still active in 2019 on Twitter, tweeting about Major League Lacrosse and the hopeful return of the Hounds in the near future.

"Fan groups like that are great for the sport," Crowley said. "They make being a professional lacrosse player that much better. They add to the experience. Playing in Charlotte, we had a great stadium, we had pretty good crowds, and we had a great team."

After three seasons in Charlotte, Crowley inked a new three-year contract with the Hounds in December of 2018, a couple months before Charlotte ceased operations, making it three teams Crowley played for that no longer existed.

"It's unfortunate that team wasn't able to stay together because I think we would've won some championships. We had a lot of young talent, a lot of great pieces there," he said. "It sucks. We have Hounds group chats through Snapchat that guys post memories on. It's interesting to see that stuff. It's a weird experience."

It's an experience Kaut could relate to. He was drafted into Major League Lacrosse in 2014 by the Boston Cannons and was acquired by the Florida Launch the following year. In 2016, his second season with Florida, Kaut became the starting goaltender.

Having played for Florida and having made memories in his career against the Hounds and Machine, Kaut agreed it is weird for those teams to no longer exist, but he was optimistic those things happened for a reason.

"The league changes. Things get better. Things get worse," he said. "It's always on the up and up, so the league is doing it for reasons for growth: the growth of the sport and growth of the league. They're making the right decisions. It's great to see. There's definitely a growth coming very soon, so it's nice to see."

The Lizards had a major need at the goalie position heading into the 2019 season as Drew Adams, the team's starting goaltender every year since 2010, joined the PLL. Ironically, Kaut, a Pennsylvania-native, was a protégé of Adams, who also was from Pennsylvania. He also trained under Brian Dougherty. Dougherty's time in Major League Lacrosse and with the Philadelphia Barrage was an early inspiration for Kaut.

"Going to their camps and clinics my entire life and becoming a fan, living in Philadelphia and being a fan of the Philadelphia Barrage and watching them win championship after championship was a kid's dream to watch those guys and watch your mentors do their thing on the field every day," he said. "You want to strive to be that type of player and get to be that level of play."

Bayhawks goalie Niko Amato, also a Pennsylvania-native and frequenter of Barrage games, was behind Kaut on the depth chart for a year in Florida. He had plenty of complimentary things to say about Kaut.

"He's a really nice guy. He's a great goalie," said Amato. "To be honest, I think we're both pretty competitive on the field, but it's a healthy competition. After every game, we've been able to put our pride to the side and shake hands and congratulate each other on our successes."

Getting to Major League Lacrosse may have seemed like the hardest part of being a professional lacrosse player, but Kaut learned quickly that staying in the league might be harder.

As a rookie, Kaut played in only four games and for a total of 53 minutes. After changing teams the following year, he still spent most of the season on the bench, playing in only five games. Not only did he have to adjust to better shooters and different defenses, he also had to adjust to the travel challenges of being a professional lacrosse player, and those didn't end once he became an established player in the league.

"I had [a bad travel story] last season when I was playing with the Launch," he said. "My flight from Philadelphia got delayed. I tried to get a connector down to Washington and then up to Ohio to go play in Ohio. My connector got out of Philly to Washington, and then my Washington flight to Ohio got cancelled, and there were no more flights going out because of the storm, so I had to call a buddy that lives 15 to 20 minutes from the airport, stayed at his place, went back to the airport in the morning, flew in, walked right on the field to walk through, took one or two shots with no chest protector just to see the ball, went to the game, and ended up having 25 saves that night against Ohio in a win.

"You have to have the mental aspect that the travel can't affect you, and do your thing and play your game," he added. "You're here for a reason. You just have to keep playing."

The travel and many team changes hadn't deterred Crowley, either.

"It's never been to a point where this is too much for me," he said. "I just love it, so I'm going to do it until my body falls apart."

Being a professional made all the obstacles worth it for Crowley and Kaut. Even though the stands weren't as full as other sports, there were many youngsters in the crowd that admired and looked up to the players. Kaut wanted to make sure he can make their day.

"That's where it kind of comes down to why I do it and why I take pride in it after every game, whether it's home or away, to talk to the fans," he said. "I knew I was in those shoes one day, and I always wanted them to come over and sign something, talk to me, and it's where I got it, from seeing those guys back in the day do that and kind of talk to the crowd and converse.

"After every game, you try to talk to the fans and the little kids in the stands that are in fourth grade and starting to play goalie," he said. "I didn't start playing goalie until eighth grade, so it's kind of great to see these guys starting at a younger age and hopefully kind of guide them in the right path to put the work in outside of practice to get them a scholarship to college and then, hopefully, to the professional league one day."

Not only did the Lizards add three All-Stars in the off-season, they also added a coach with a championship pedigree: B.J. O'Hara. He had just come off a season where he helped lead the Denver Outlaws to their third championship. O'Hara was the coach for all of those championship teams, the first coach to win three championships with one team. He also was the first coach with four championships overall, winning one with the Rochester Rattlers in 2008. He came into the season with a regular season record of 81-67 and a playoff record of 9-4.

With all of the impressive additions, the fans had lofty expectations for the Lizards, expectations the team did not live up to.

New York lost its first four games of the season and suffered a five-game losing streak beginning August 3, which included a 24-7 home loss to the Bayhawks on August 4.

"We certainly were honest with the guys in terms of where we were coming up short. We also tried to be positive and look for things we could improve on," O'Hara said. "It's tough in this league because you don't have five practices a week. You don't have film meetings and stuff like that. We do film, but we do it remotely. We'll look at every aspect of what I'm doing, what the assistants are doing. I've said a lot this year, it's not what we're doing; it's how we're doing it, what kind of energy we're playing with, what kind of commitment we're doing."

But for one night, it seemed as if the team figured things out, giving fans a glimpse of what they had hoped for, and Kaut was a big reason for it.

After Pannell scored the first goal of the game, the Atlanta Blaze scored three consecutive goals to take the lead. With 29 seconds remaining in the first quarter, former Lizard Tommy Palasek scored his third goal of the quarter and gave the playoff-bound Blaze a 6-4 lead. The Lizards ran an offensive set, but came away empty-handed, and with six seconds remaining, the Blaze defense heaved the ball down the field in a seemingly safe move.

Kaut caught the ball and sent it right back with roughly two seconds remaining. The ball went over the sticks of the Blaze defense and past a surprised Chris Madalon for a two-point goal.

"It was a little bit of luck," Kaut said. "I saw there was a little bit of time left. With the new rule, if it leaves your stick before the clock's out, it's good if it goes. I just tried to chuck it down there and hope it went, and it happened to go."

The goal tied the game at six, putting the team right back in contention.

Kaut was a presence again in the second quarter when he came out of his crease to lay out Atlanta rookie T.J. Comizio. The Blaze scored on the play, but the big hit showed the Lizards were not going to go down without a fight (literally, three and a half minutes later, a scrum broke out between the two teams that sent four players into the penalty box).

In the third quarter, down 12-9, the Lizards offense erupted, scoring six consecutive goals, including two from Molloy and one apiece from Pannell and Crowley, giving the Lizards back the lead. The team opened things up in the fourth quarter, outscoring Atlanta 5-2 in the quarter and winning the regular season finale, 21-15.

Pannell finished with a game-high eight points on five goals and three assists; Molloy had four goals and one assist, Crowley added two goals, and Kaut finished with 15 saves, three ground balls, and the two-point goal.

"Rob had his best game," O'Hara said. "We feed off of him. He's had a good year, but he had a great game tonight. Kevin Crowley really started to fit in and feel comfortable. He had a great game last week. He had a good night tonight. The pieces came together. I was happy for them."

As the players celebrated after the final whistle, O'Hara watched through watery eyes.

"I'm really happy for these guys, that they could go home tonight with a good taste in their mouth and feeling good," he said. "It was a difficult situation. We had a whole new team, a whole new coaching staff. It's always a learning process getting to know each other and getting to know your teammates. For whatever reasons, we were grasping at straws a lot early on, trying to find that right mix. We played well a lot; we only had a couple games we really didn't compete well. Mostly every game, we were there. We just had a lot of trouble finishing them. Tonight, we finished."

And with that, the 2019 MLL regular season was finished as well.

8.
OCTOBER 6
MLL CHAMPIONSHIP WEEKEND

Lyle Thompson: Ron Chenoy/Pretty Instant

At the conclusion of the MLL regular season, the Chesapeake Bayhawks finished at the top of the standings with a 10-6 record. Joining the Bayhawks in the postseason were the second-seeded defending champion Denver Outlaws, the third-seeded Boston Cannons (playing in the playoffs for the first time since 2015 and only the second time in the past seven seasons), and the fourth-seeded Atlanta Blaze (making the playoffs for the first time in franchise history). The Rattlers, winless through the first seven games of the season, made a remarkable run back to relevancy, winning six consecutive games before losing two of their final three games of the regular season. At the bottom of the table was the New York Lizards, who finished 5-11 but won two of the final three games of the year.

The format for the 2019 playoffs returned to the version where the semi-finals and championship game were played in the same host city over the course of the same weekend; this was a change from the previous five seasons where the league played a two-week playoff format where the higher-seeded teams hosted the semi-final game, and the championship game was played at a neutral site the following weekend.

On July 15, the league announced Denver would host MLL Championship Weekend, with Denver University the site for the semi-final games and Dick's Sporting Goods Park (home of MLS's Colorado Rapids) the site for the championship game two days later. This meant that although the Chesapeake Bayhawks had the best regular season, the second-seeded Denver Outlaws would have home-field advantage throughout the playoffs.

The semifinals proved to be exciting theatre, showcasing the parity in the league.

In the first semi-final, the Chesapeake Bayhawks defeated the Atlanta Blaze, 14-13, in overtime. The Blaze led for a majority of the game, including a 4-3 lead at the end of the first quarter followed by a 5-1 run in the second quarter, giving Atlanta a 9-4 lead heading into halftime; the defense even held virtuoso attackman Lyle Thompson, the top scorer in the league (a league-best 46 goals to go with 27 assists), in check, yielding only two assists to Thompson in the first half. Chesapeake came alive in the second half, however, scoring seven of the first eight goals of the half. Steele Stanwick scored the game-winning goal in overtime to send Chesapeake to its first championship game since 2013.

In the second semi-final, the higher-seeded team again got off to an equally slow start. The Boston Cannons jumped on the Outlaws quickly, ending the first quarter with a 7-3 lead. Denver rallied in the second quarter, scoring seven goals, but Boston still held a 13-10 advantage. The Outlaws defense closed the door on the Cannons in the second half, however, allowing only one goal in each of the final two quarters and coming back to win, 17-15. Rookie Chris Aslanian tied for the team lead in scoring with four goals – including the game-winner at the 5:41 mark – and one assist. Aslanian's veteran teammate, John Grant Jr., scored five goals.

The championship showdown was set; the top two teams in the 2019 standings, as well as the two-best teams in league history in number of championships and championship appearances (Denver's three championship wins were tied for second-most in league history with the New York Lizards and the then-defunct Philadelphia Barrage), would square off in the final game of the season.

Before a champion was crowned, however, individual awards would be handed out at the MLL Honors the night between the semifinals and championship game. The award ceremony was held at Denver Union Station. As guests arrived in the spacious downtown venue, Denver Outlaws cheerleaders led them down the red-carpet.

There was food, drink, music, and socializing, but the main event was to reveal the award winners. Denver's Tony Seaman won the league's Coach of the Year award; Chesapeake's Ryan Tucker won the Corum Player's Choice Award, given to the player considered "the best teammate" and voted on by the players; Boston's Nick Marrocco was selected by a panel of voters as the David Huntley Man of the Year; Atlanta's Liam Byrnes and Alex Woodall were named Defensive Player of the Year and Rookie of the Year, respectively; and Chesapeake's Lyle Thompson was named the Offensive Player of the Year and league MVP.

The only player who was not on a playoff team that won an individual award was Dallas rookie Sean Sconone, who was named the league's Goaltender of the Year.

As the Denver Outlaws and Chesapeake Bayhawks battled in the Championship Game the afternoon after MLL Honors, Sconone sat high above the field, in the area reserved for press, taking in the game as a spectator. He was at the game but not in the role he hoped for.

"We should be out here as a team," Sconone said. "Two one-goal games at the end of the season really killed us. When we were going, we were tough to beat."

For the first half of the season, it would be hard to believe someone when they said the Rattlers should be in the championship game, but the team's six-game winning streak, which included five victories over the four playoff teams (including two over the Outlaws), made that statement more legitimate.

There were a number of reasons for Dallas's turnaround, but the wins coincided with the beginning of Sconone's tenure starting between the pipes. The undrafted rookie free agent from the University of Massachusetts-Amherst was picked up by the Rattlers and head coach Bill Warder on June 6. On June 27, he made his MLL debut and first start in an away game against the Denver Outlaws.

"That's how I knew it was real," he said, "playing in a football stadium."

Dallas lost that game and the next three to go to 0-7 on the season. The Rattlers then returned to Denver for a game on July 21, the final weekend before the All-Star break.

On paper, it should have been a lopsided affair; the undefeated, defending champion Outlaws – who were one of the league's top offenses – against the winless Rattlers, who were starting a rookie goaltender. That's the thing about sports, though; games aren't played on paper, and players have to execute on the field and earn the victory. That day, Sconone made 20 saves and Dallas beat Denver, 11-8.

That was the start of Dallas's impressive streak. By the end of the season, Sconone led the league in save percentage (55.81 percent) and goals against average (12.09). An article on the MLL website, written by MLL intern Tyler Englander, was published on August 19 with the title "Sean Sconone: The Man That Saved the Rattlers Season."

"What Sean brings is a tremendous amount of stability and quality of goaltending," Warder said. "The baseball stat is wins above replacement. It's hard to equate there's someone who's given us more wins than he has so far."

Sconone had never been to Dallas before he was picked up by the Rattlers. He said the travel took some time getting used to, especially coming from New York, but once he got his routine down, flying over the weekend was "another business trip."

He was not on anybody's radar at the start of the MLL season, but by the end of it, he was the talk of the town. For him, it was a dream come true.

"It's a great group of guys in the MLL," he said. "The guys up for the [Goalie of the Year] award were deserving. All these guys are really good goalies. To be part of that is something really amazing. Being up there [at MLL Honors] with guys like Lyle Thompson and to see John Grant at the awards, it's really awesome. Growing up, you're watching John Grant as a kid. Being up there with him, shaking his hand, was a cool experience."

The start of the MLL Championship Game was not a cool experience for the Denver Outlaws. Despite the announced crowd of 6,374 people overwhelmingly in support of the local team, the beginning of the game belonged to the Chesapeake Bayhawks. The Bayhawks scored the first five goals of the game, and the defense shut down the vaunted Denver offense, holding it to only three goals in the entire first half, taking an 8-3 lead into halftime.

"We played this team two and three weeks ago," head coach Dave Cottle said. "We had an idea what we wanted to do."

Despite the large lead and momentum, as the semifinals showed, no lead was safe in Major League Lacrosse. Chesapeake's defense was stout in the first half, but it was time for the Denver defense to shine in the second half. Denver shut out Chesapeake in the third quarter and started a run of its own. With 7:52 remaining in the fourth quarter, Ryan Lee scored to give Denver a 9-8 lead, its first of the game.

"There's so many flows in this game," Chesapeake long-stick midfielder C.J. Costabile said. "Even when we played the Blaze the other day, Denver when they played the Cannons, this is a game of runs. It's how you respond to those runs that's really going to dictate how you're able to perform going forward."

The fourth quarter was frantic as Denver picked up momentum and Chesapeake tried to hold on. The game was all hands on deck, doing whatever was needed to win the game. Matt Abbott, a two-way midfielder for the Bayhawks, even took a long-pole and played on defense in a man-down situation.

Finally, after Chesapeake was held scoreless for nearly 30 minutes, and more than five minutes after Lee's goal to give Denver the lead,

Steele Stanwick – the hero of Friday's semifinal game – scored to tie the game at nine. Nick Mariano drew the attention of two Denver defenders at the top of the two-point arc, and a third was caught ball-watching, giving Stanwick a few yards of separation. Mariano passed the ball to Stanwick, who drove to the crease and dove across it, putting the ball in the back of the net before landing.

That offensive set not only tied the game, it also put the Outlaws at a severe disadvantage. Denver players were frustrated with officials because they believed Stanwick made contact with Outlaws goalie Dillon Ward during his dive, which would have nullified the goal; the play was reviewed and upheld. Two Denver players were also called for penalties – including top defenseman Finn Sullivan, who was flagged for a high-hit on Colin Heacock (who had passed the ball to Mariano on the equalizer) – putting the team down two men.

Bayhawks faceoff specialist Kenny Massa won the ensuing faceoff, and on the offensive possession, the ball got to Stanwick behind the cage. He found rookie Andrew Kew on the right wing, and Kew scored with 1:11 remaining, putting the Bayhawks ahead, 10-9. Massa won the next faceoff, and Chesapeake was able to finish off the game and win the championship.

"It's a culmination of so many things," Costabile said. "You think about the journey. It starts in May of this year, practicing, training camp. It's a long season this year, playing lacrosse all the way to October. We just never played a game fully to 60 minutes. This is the first time I feel we fully played to our capabilities. Going through a little lull offensively in the second half, we hunkered down on defense, and we were able to finish out to take the W at the end."

As Chesapeake's players celebrated on the field, the Bayhawks logo was the image on all of the championship shirts and hats. It took a team – particularly one like the Bayhawks that had a number of returning veterans like Abbott, Costabile, Phipps, Amato, and Jesse Bernhardt – to win the championship. The face of the 2019 MLL season, however, was Lyle Thompson.

Thompson was one of the most popular players in NCAA lacrosse when he was at Albany (surprising as it was to not play for a school like Syracuse, Johns Hopkins, Virginia, or Duke). He was a two-time Tewaaraton Award winner, one of only two players in the history of the award to do so. He set the NCAA Division 1 records for career points (400) and assists (225), and he did it with a litany of SportsCenter worthy plays.

He was selected first overall by the Florida Launch in the 2015 MLL Collegiate Draft. While he provided moments of brilliance, Thompson never had the same season-long impact in MLL that he did in NCAA. The answer why it never happened was simple: he never played a full season.

From 2015 to 2018, Thompson never played more than nine games in a season due to the overlap between MLL and NLL (where he won the championship and league MVP with the Georgia Swarm in 2017). In 2018, between overlaps with the NLL and FIL World Championships, Thompson played in only three MLL games that season.

Prior to the 2019 season, Lyle's brother, Miles, and his cousins, Jeremy and Ty, moved from the MLL to the PLL, and many fans assumed Lyle would do so as well. In 2017, however, Lyle had signed a contract extension with MLL and the Bayhawks that would keep him with Chesapeake through 2021. With the start of the MLL season moving from April to June, the overlap between MLL and NLL was removed, meaning the team and league would get a full season of Lyle Thompson.

He did not disappoint. Thompson led the league in points and goals. He was the captain of one of the two All-Star teams.

"He was the best player in the league," Bayhawks head coach Dave Cottle said about him.

The fans adored him.

At the July 20 game against the New York Lizards, young lacrosse players were invited down to the field to form a tunnel and high-five Bayhawks players as they were announced onto the field. When Thompson was announced, he made it halfway through the line before the tunnel collapsed into a mob of children surrounding him.

That same day, in the midst of a heat wave, Thompson spent the morning and afternoon in three different media sessions as well as an autograph signing.

"Sometimes, it's overwhelming," he said, "but for the most part, I just try to be there for the fans as much as possible."

Even opponents were amazed by him.

"He's unguardable," Outlaws attackman John Grant Jr. said after

Denver played Chesapeake on the Fourth of July. "Clearly, if he's not the best player in the world, he's definitely in the top three. And unfortunately, watching him do it against my team is tough, but a dazzling player to watch. The league is very, very lucky to have a guy like that."

All the attention Thompson received could be distracting for his team or cause some to get jealous, but his teammates share the admiration for Thompson, and most of it is because of how humble and unselfish he is.

"He's a freak," Costabile said. "The beauty of him is he's not one of those players who does it himself, and it's just about him. He really is a guy who makes everyone around him better. He'll draw the slide. He'll move it one more when it comes down. He's a crunch time player. He wants the ball. He's demanding, and he gets it done. People feed off his energy."

"I'm very happy he is on our team," long-stick midfielder Jesse Bernhardt said. "For a guy who puts up such highlight reel goals, he is a true team player. He puts up a ton of team points. He is always looking to distribute the ball. He knows himself. He knows he draws a lot of attention."

Championship Weekend added more hardware for Thompson to add to his trophy case, winning the MLL Offensive Player of the Year award, MVP award, and MLL Championship. In the final, he scored two goals and added an assist, tying for the game-high in points.

For all the individual attention he received and success he enjoyed, it was being able to celebrate a victory with his team – which he said came together "as a family" – that was most important to him.

"At the end of the day, that's the team effort. That's the team goal," he said about what the championship meant to him. "Me, personally, I try to stay in the moment every game I play, whether it's a championship game and the game's on the line or it's midseason and it's a blow-out. The opportunity to play is what I'm truly thankful for. It may sound a little silly to a lot of people, but a championship is no bigger than the next game or the last game. I try to live in the moment and enjoy the process, enjoy every day and this moment."

While the Bayhawks players celebrated in front of the goal, hugging each other, talking, and taking pictures with the trophy, as the fans exited the stadium, Alexander "Sandy" Brown stood off to the side, quietly watching.

Brown was the commissioner of Major League Lacrosse, and the 2019 season was his second in charge. He was hired in February of 2018 as the second commissioner in league history, succeeding David Gross. He arrived in the league after the data breach that exposed personal information of active and retired players; he arrived after the league announced the Rochester Rattlers were moving to Dallas; he arrived after the league partnered with Lax Sports Network and put all of its games behind a paywall. All of those scenarios left fans and players with a poor taste in their mouths, nor was it an ideal situation for a new leader to walk into.

Brown was up for the challenge, however. He was a successful sports executive; he was the President and CEO of One World Sports, a sports cable channel and over-the-top platform, prior to taking the position with MLL. From 2010 through 2012, he was the President of Sports at Univision. Other notable previous positions were as the television sales manager for NBA International from 1990 to 1992 and the managing director of both ESPN Asia and ESPN Star Sports.

Maybe more importantly, Brown knew and liked lacrosse. He played collegiately for Washington and Lee University (the same place Bryant University head coach Mike Pressler played) and played in the 1985 USILA North South Game.

He was tested right in the beginning of his first MLL season. In the first game the Rattlers played in Dallas (the second week of the 2018 season), the clock malfunctioned multiple times causing stoppages in play, including during overtime. Brown responded by tweeting, "Today was not the @MLL_Lacrosse's best effort. A series of clock/game management mishaps in the @RattlersLax and @DenverOutlaws game in Dallas marred what was an outstanding and hard fought game between two excellent lacrosse teams. We owe everyone much better, and we will." The tweet didn't have much feedback (it was retweeted three times, liked 29 times, and replied to three times), but the replies were favorable, making a point to appreciate the commissioner for owning up to the mistakes.

As the season progressed, the reviews weren't always as supportive. Only a few weeks later, Ryan Flanagan, then a defender for the New York Lizards, sent a tweet that read, "No locker room. No showers. Pizza and Beer post-game. HUGE @LizardsLacrosse W!

#WelcomeToTheLeague." Flanagan was fined a game check for his comment. He responded by tweeting, "Today I was notified by @MLL_Lacrosse that @MLLCommish has fined me a complete game check for a tweet I posted on Saturday night. The tweet that was sent stated facts surrounding our teams experience and expresses enthusiasm in our teams ability to overcome adversity as a group." Despite the explanation of what Flanagan viewed as less-than-professional amenities, it did not change the status of the fine.

After a second off-season that included the emergence of competition in the PLL (which included over 100 players leaving MLL) and the folding of three teams, Brown's job did not get easier in season two.

Despite the controversy, Brown was pleased with how his second season in charge transpired.

"We made a lot of internal changes this year in terms of structural changes that were really important for us to get new teams into the league," he said after the championship game. "We changed our season. We added to the roster size. We're playing in October. I think we looked at the month of September as data to see is this really going to work or not, and I've got to tell you, the concept of having the final four this weekend, I couldn't be happier. After the Honors show last night, I said, 'Well, we're three for four. Let's see what happens today.' I think we hit the bid. I was very, very happy with what happened this weekend."

Brown saw Championship Weekend as a huge success because of how it showcased the competition and talent the league had. All three of the games played Championship Weekend were one-possession games and featured come-from-behind victories; two games were decided by one goal, and one went to overtime.

In what seemed like a trend the league couldn't shake, however, with positive came negative. In addition to the complaints about the officiating in the MLL Championship Game, there were grumblings that despite Chesapeake being the top-seed in the playoffs, the championship game was played in the home city of its opponent, the Denver Outlaws. Major League Lacrosse reported the attendance at the final was 6,374 people, and most were rooting for the hometown Outlaws. While the announcement Denver would host Championship Weekend came in mid-July, and there was no knowledge what seed the Outlaws would earn or that they would even make it that far, what made the decision slightly more odd was of the six championships played from 2013 through 2018, only once did the league play in a city that was home to one of the teams in the league.

Even if he wasn't complaining, Bayhawks head coach Dave Cottle said the crowd was definitely an advantage for the Outlaws.

"We're playing it on the road at Denver," he said. "When things went against us, the crowd really helped them. I thought they did a great job cheering on their team."

Brown, however, looked at the situation more glass half-full.

"That's what we want," he said. "We want fans that are engaged. We're all engaged with the players and coaches and owners and the league, and we want our fans engaged, and they came and showed it today. This league is all about the fans. That's job one, two, and three for us. It's not about anything other than them. The fans allow us to be able to do what we do here, and our job is to make sure we put on the best show we possibly can."

A month after the 2019 MLL season concluded, the league put out multiple press releases highlighting development the league made in 2019. According to those releases: the league saw a 16 percent increase in total attendance year-over-year, signed 10 new partnerships, and generated 194 percent growth in social traffic as well as 97 percent growth in social engagement and 393 percent growth in web traffic. Additionally, three teams (Boston, Dallas, and Denver) fielded youth teams, and the league reached 724 million viewers through national and regional broadcast deals.

Even without those numbers at his disposal immediately after the championship game, Brown was very happy with the direction of both the league and the sport.

"We had John Grant Jr. coming back. He was phenomenal today; he was phenomenal Friday night; he's been phenomenal all year. That's a tremendous story," he said. "We had a great new venue in Boston. Rob Hale has done a superb job in what the Cannons have done this year. Two weekends ago, we had two of our venues at capacity. You had the World Indoors [championship tournament], you had the PLL championship, and you had the NLL draft all in September. My view is the growth of the sport, this is a train that's not going to stop. I am more excited than ever about what we're seeing. When you look at the quality of play in the athletes we saw on the field today, it's mind boggling. It's been fun growing up, playing this game, and to see the level of play continue to grow and continue to get better and better that you see today."

Through 19 seasons, the league, its players, its coaches, and its fans experienced a multitude of ups and downs.

When everything comes together, however, being a part of something special is worth the hectic travel, the busy summers, the unforeseen missteps, and the negativity on social media.

"The beauty of this group is everyone is about the team effort here," Bayhawks defender C.J. Costabile said. "Yesterday, we had guys winning awards, some great awards, [Ryan] Tucker winning teammate of the year, Lyle winning his awards, but at the end of the day, I tell you, you look at all those guys in the face, they would give that all up in a heartbeat to win a championship. It just goes to show how close-knit this group is.

"It's tough," he added. "When you play in the MLL, it's very different than when you get to play college. (In college) you practice with these guys, you go out with them, you do everything. Here, you're practicing once a week and you're playing on a Saturday, so you have to figure out team chemistry in a short amount of time. That's also why you have so many guys here for so long, because of the culture here."

FINAL WORDS

If fortune and fame aren't part of the equation, why do the Major League Lacrosse players end a busy, tiring workday by going to the gym, throwing against a wall, and watching film, all on their own? Why, at the end of the week, when they could spend time with their families and friends, do they put up with flight cancellations and lost baggage in order to play a game that, in many cases, is not how they support their families?

Why do the MLL players, coaches, and fans care so much and remain invested in a league that some denigrate, and many others are unaware of?

Pride. Passion. Chasing a dream. Accomplishing a goal. Commitment. Inspiring others to realize a positive path they could go down in the future. Family and camaraderie. Love of the game.

The players, coaches, and fans want to be a part of a community, a part of something bigger than themselves. They want to be a part of something that was there before them and, after 19 seasons and counting, they hope will be even better for others when they're gone.

ABOUT THE AUTHOR

Brett Davis/Pretty Instant

Phil Shore has covered lacrosse since 2010 for publications such as *The Boston Globe, New England Lacrosse Journal,* and *US Lacrosse Magazine.* He also hosted a live, online radio show for Lacrosse Radio Network called *Lacrosse Lounge.*

Shore played lacrosse collegiately at Emerson College, where he earned his B.S. in Print and Multimedia Journalism. In addition to his writing responsibilities, Shore is a high school lacrosse coach and a middle school language arts teacher.

Made in the USA
Middletown, DE
22 June 2020

10717952R00073